War
In the
Spirit Realm

By
Betty Swinford

Hidden Manna Publications

War In the Spirit Realm

Copyright © 2023 by Gentle Shepherd
Ministries

ISBN: 978-8-9893588-0-9

Except where otherwise indicated, all Scripture quotations in this book are taken from the King James Version.

Hidden Manna Publications
P.O. Box 3572
Oldtown, ID 83822
www.gentleshepherd.com

Facebook:
https://www.facebook.com/HiddenMannaPublications/

Contents

INTRODUCTION

The book you hold in your hands has a history. You can almost relate it to the born-again experience. Like the new-birth experience for the Christian, this book was brought forth through great travail wrought out of extreme testing, an intense spiritual struggle, and experiences that resulted in an incredible testimony. The original manuscript was produced on a typewriter and sent through the mail to a book agent, only to somehow become lost in the midst of the conglomeration of the Postal Service.

Even though it was thought to be lost and gone forever, as with all great truths, it was preserved by the author in the form of cassette tapes. A studious Bible student by the name of Kitty Miller actually transcribed the tapes, and then, years later, her transcript was scanned and edited for publication by Jeannette Haley who was a personal friend of the author, Betty Swinford.

To those of the present era, the history of this book may seem archaic, but the truths and experiences recorded in it are not. God has not changed, Satan's devices remain the same but are adjusted according to the present darkness invading the times we live in, and man's spiritual plight remains unchanged. He is lost until he truly becomes born again of the Holy Spirit and the washing of the water of the Word of God.

The form of ministry mentioned in it will seem foreign to those who were not part of the great moves of God during the 1970's-80's when certain evangelists actually cast strong shadows among even the various counterfeits who were trying to ride in on the waves of this movement. These spiritual giants left an indelible witness. Betty Swinford was one of those anointed

5

evangelists that touched countless lives during her many years of ministry.

Betty never shied away from taking on controversial subjects that were treated as taboo in the church. She ministered where the door opened to her such as in Catholic churches, but never wavered from the Gospel message. She admittedly gained insight from controversial people who were considered questionable in their beliefs and practices, and mystics, but through it all she always came back to the Word of God and knew how to properly discern the person and work of the Holy Spirit.

One such subject Betty became well acquainted with was the bizarre realm of Satan. The Apostle Paul told us we are not to be ignorant of his devices, but when it comes to the church in America, we not only chose to be ignorant, but we hide behind that ignorance while claiming some type of immunity from being affected by Satan as are other pagan cultures in their idolatry and practices.

As believers, we are to be soldiers who realize we do not fight against flesh and blood but against the unseen realm of darkness. The battle is spiritual and to be victorious we have been given an armor in which to stand, a weapon with which to push the enemy back, and authority in prayer to ensure his defeat.

For ministers on the front line, it is not unusual to encounter the influence, working, and ways of Satan. To ignore it is destructive, to downplay it means defeat, and to mock it will prove to be utter foolishness in the end. It is for this reason that when the devices of Satan are encountered, he is usually ignored and rarely confronted because people fail to discern him and as a result, he does not have to flee.

When Betty passed away in 2007, she was aware of others who were attempting to revive this information and see it in published form without any success. In a joint effort we are now resurrecting this book and are excited about making this information available to those who know the victorious Christian life has been elusive for too long. It is time to take a stand upon truth, withstand with faith and continue to stand because the Lord has promised us not only an overcoming, victorious life, but an abundant one that is full and complete.

We have also added Betty's excellent booklet *The Word of Knowledge* to this publication for the edification of others. She copyrighted this small booklet in 1976, the year I was saved. She published it herself because publishers were uninterested in the subject. Once again, she wrote a thorough presentation and we did not want the information to be left buried and unavailable to the Body of Christ. Hence, we have resurrected it to reveal her insights, while maintaining the precious legacy she has left behind.

**Publisher
Rayola Kelley**

Chapter 1

DISCERNING OF SPIRITS

In *I Corinthians 12:10* we read, *"To another the working of miracles; to another prophecy; to another discerning of spirits; to another divers kinds of tongues; to another the interpretation of tongues."*

What is discerning of Spirits? It is a gift given by the Holy Spirit to enable one to see into and beyond the physical. It is a light that shines into the dark corridors of the soul. It is not ESP or divination, and it is not the "gift of suspicion".

It is a clear directive from the Holy Spirit to see into lives and detect the presence of evil spirits. It is not being judgmental or critical. The Christian who is able to discern is often misunderstood and his knowledge often rejected. Many times, he is forced to stand alone waiting for God to confirm what he has been shown. Inwardly he wonders that what is so clear to him is overlooked by others.

This is how it works: never speak lightly of this gift. It is the Holy Spirit taking the things of God and showing them to you. Jesus said in *John 16:15, "All things that the Father hath are mine: therefore said I, that he shall take of mine, and shall shew it unto you."* Never ignore what God is showing you. You can trust the Holy Spirit within you.

Discerning may operate differently through different individuals. For instance, one person may be in the presence of an evil spirit and get sick to his stomach, another may feel bad vibes like invisible rays coming at him, and still others may look into the eyes of one who has a wrong spirit and actually identify that spirit; remember, the eyes are the windows of the soul.

Every spirit has a different look. A tormenting spirit does not look like a lying spirit. A spirit of lust does not look like a spirit of fear. Only the teaching of the Holy Spirit can show one the various spirits that are at work in people's lives. If for instance you are in the presence of person who has a spirit of lust, you may sense sudden unexplainable sexual urges. It will almost always prove out that the person you are with has a spirit of lust. Or perhaps you are talking with someone and suddenly you get very nervous. You don't want to look at that person or be with them. What you really want to do is flee from their presence. You have just encountered a nervous spirit.

An individual with a tormenting, confused spirit will affect you so that it is hard to think. You begin to feel thickheaded, confused, and your thoughts are in disarray. The spirit in the other person is leaning his presence against you.

We are spirit beings; essentially, that's what we are. We have to have bodies or we would be invisible. So, when we meet with friends, relatives or strangers we are not merely meeting flesh and bones, we are meeting a spirit. Paul admonished us to know no man after the flesh (*2 Corinthians 5:16*). He said again in *Ephesians 6:12*, *"For we wrestle not against flesh & blood, but against principalities, against powers against the rulers of the darkness of this world, against spiritual wickedness in high places."*

Many gullible souls have been deceived because of their lack of spiritual discernment. It is important that when we meet with people, we are able to sift through what is being said to what actually is. The cults are filled with those who instead of checking out the spirits were pulled in hook, line and sinker: blinded to facts and truth. John said in *I John 4:2-3,*

> *Hereby know you the Spirit of God: Every spirit that confesses that Jesus Christ is come in the flesh is of God: And every spirit that confesses not that Jesus Christ is come in the flesh is not of God: and this is that spirit of anti-Christ, whereof you have heard that it should come; and even now already it is in the world.*

God doesn't want us to accept things at face value. He wants us to check out the speakers we hear, the people we meet, and the situations that smack of evil. That is not to say that we read people, this is shameful and disgusting. When a true spirit of discerning is present there is never a need to try and read into people, the gift will work for itself.

Satan hates and fears this gift. Discernment uncovers the activity of Satan and probes into his kingdom. He cannot tolerate such involvement from the Christian and will do everything in his power to backup such a person. He wants his deeds kept under wraps and will retaliate, if possible, when his works are illuminated. He will join in the chorus already being sung that the believer is critical and judgmental. He will try to oppress the one who has discernment with wicked spirits who lean their presence against him and will oppose him in every way. He will threaten, bluff and roar at that believer who has escaped his stronghold and now holds the keys that can spell his defeat.

Example: I suspected Wilma had an evil spirit and that she was in need of deliverance. I put my discernment on the "back burner" waiting for God to vindicate her. During a solemn time of prayer, Wilma disrupted the communion service with an out loud conversation with God and no one admonished her. On the way

11

to prayer in the evening, Wilma confessed she felt like she had a demon by her own admission.

Example: The man leading the singing had a spirit of deception. At a time for testimony, the first person up was the song leader and he began to thank God for not being in deception and thanked God for not being a phony. The devil knew that my husband and I knew what spirit he had.

Example: There was a woman who lived in the country in a cluttered house with a very large collection of ceramic pigs, salt and pepper shakers, and pictures of pigs, etc. all throughout the house. There was oppression in the house. The sick lady was a very heavy-set woman who looked like a sow lying on her side in a pigsty. This woman literally had the spirit of a pig and it was everywhere present in that home. This woman, somewhere along the way, had given herself over to such a spirit.

Example: Lucy had been seeking help, but had been turned away by many people. The Holy Spirit came upon her and she fell under the power of God. She was screaming and throwing herself on the floor and the pastor did not recognize that this was not the Spirit of God. She was partially delivered.

The Holy Spirit does not scream and writhe and twist. He may shout, but does not scream. These are important facts to keep in mind when identifying evil spirits.

Discernment is not a show-off gift. It is never to be used in exalting an individual. Spiritual discernment is serious business and should be treated as such. For instance, a pastor should never tell someone that they have a wrong spirit unless he is prepared at that time to cast it out. No one should be picked out of a congregation and told that he or she is possessed, you can destroy a life that way. Besides, it is embarrassing and it can do irreparable harm to the individual in front of other people.

Never go overboard and begin thinking that everything is a demon. There is not a demon behind every bush or under every rock. Self-styled demon chasers are dangerous people and often do more harm than they do good. Some self-appointed demon chasers are sincere, but misguided and believe that every Christian is in need of deliverance. They can scar people for life.

There are those who are demon hunters: be careful for it can be a very dangerous game. Do not chase after demons, but do pray earnestly for this gift to operate in your life. In this day of false teachers and false prophets the ability to discern good from evil is needed as never before.

A spirit of revelation: This is a "Siamese twin" for both discerning of spirits and the word of knowledge. It comes swiftly as though someone flipped a light switch. In one blinding flash you know everything about an individual and this knowledge is almost always accompanied with a mental picture. The Bible says, *"That the God of our Lord Jesus Christ, the Father of glory, may give unto you the spirit of wisdom and revelation in the knowledge of him"* (Ephesians 1:17-18). The Living Bible says the eyes of your heart being flooded with light and that is exactly what it is.

Personal Experience: I was staying in the home of a pastor when the pastor's "right-hand man" arrived on the scene. The Holy Spirit hates phoniness. Then I saw upon shaking the "right-hand man's" hand a mental picture of incest, cruelty to his wife, (especially in matters concerning sex) and a double life. I accepted the information coming from the Holy Spirit, but what to do with it? Nothing—wait until confirmation comes. God always confirms what he reveals.

13

During the meeting the son of this man came to speak to me about his father's life and how he and his sister were awakened during the night to cries from his mother. Then the daughter came home from Bible College and confided in me how she and her sister had been misused sexually.

The girl was anxious, nervous, overweight, and fearful and spoke of her older sister being in a mental institution for several years because of their father's sexual misconduct. I knew that I was on safe ground because the Spirit of God had confirmed it and now, I could go to the pastor with the information, but he did not receive it.

This is the way the spirit of revelation works. In one blinding flash you see it all. A life is totally laid bare because your spiritual eyes have been opened. If one should prematurely confide information to another individual and they would tell you that you were wrong, it would make no difference. In such cases you know that you know and no one is able to talk you out of it.

It is altogether possible for a person to come into the gift of spiritual discernment by walking with someone who already has this gift. Just by observation and taking note of what the other person points out can put one on the alert to the presence of evil spirits. After the death of my husband, a lady traveled with me. I would point out such things as the way people's eyes looked or why she felt sick to her stomach. Soon the lady had a strong ability to discern and moved on with her own ministry.

Discerning is not always so you can set one free. Seeing an evil spirit and casting it out are two entirely different things. Just because one has the ability to discern does not necessarily qualify them to cast out a demon.

Sometimes you will identify a spirit so that you can pray; sometimes it's for your own protection, other times it is so that you can warm someone. But attempting to cast out a demon without the power and anointing of the Holy Spirit can be dangerous and hard.

Example: I knew someone who tackled deliverance on a possessed individual and was thrown across the church. This man was powerful in God and knowledgeable in spiritual matters. This reminds us of the seven sons of Sceva who tried to do the same thing. They were left naked and bleeding *(Acts 19:14-16)*.

Recap: Check out the sense of ill feeling that flows up into you. Become alert when you become sick to your stomach in someone's presence. You may see another entity in the eyes of a possessed person. If one is untouchable, he has a spirit of terror. Where is that person's peace and joy? Lastly, do you have an inner witness of the spirit with that individual?

Finally, the gift of discerning of Spirits comes with a high price tag. For someone coming into this ability will first meet the spirits, battle them and overcome them. Then when they meet them again, they will know them.

It is a wonderful and worthwhile gift, and can save a person from being misled or from being otherwise duped, especially in the day in which we live. The ability to discern is urgently needed. For lack of discernment churches are split and divided and souls are brought into all sorts of bondage.

Going to the occult for power? I was staying in a Pastor's home and went to rest in the afternoon for the evening service. Within five minutes my thoughts became disoriented, jumbled, confused and just short of hallucinating. What was the problem? After all, I was in the home of a minister.

The next morning, I asked the minister who sometimes slept in that room. Surprised, he said he actually takes his naps there. I asked him, "Do you ever go through anything mental while sleeping in that bed?" and I related to him what I had experienced. At once the minister ducked his head and his wife glanced at him sharply.

He confessed he went to the occult for power for his ministry and he has never been able to shake that spirit. The very thought of going to the occult for power for ministry when the power of God is free and accessible is almost too incredulous to believe. But that is what he told me. The following morning when his wife was taking me to the airport, she shared with me the terrible nightmares and torment that he endured ever since he had opened himself up to the dark forces of the underworld.

Does an individual want to be free? This is an important and valid question, for not everyone wants to be free of the evil spirits that rule their lives.

S.S. was a member of the Christian and Missionary Alliance Church in Tucson. One year at camp an evangelist cast out of her forty demons. They literally ruled her life with everything from kleptomania to lust. Sometime later a mutual friend met S.S. and was told that S.S. let them all back in. She said, "I had them for so long I can't even make a decision without them."

Here are some pointers. Discerning of spirits, although a gift, will nevertheless cost you something. *Reason one:* You must first meet the spirits in order to be able to identify them later. *Two:* Satan will have a hatred for you and attack you when your defenses are down. Check out the things that you feel when you are with others. I reiterate, if you experience a sudden, unexplainable sexual urge you have met a spirit of lust. If you are

16

enveloped by terror that goes beyond dread, you have met a spirit of fear. If you sense a tight band around your head for no reason you have met a spirit of witchcraft or some type of the occult.

If you are with someone who makes you edgy and you want to flee their presence, you have met a nervous spirit. If you suspect a spirit of error, check them by the Word to see what it is they believe.

Like medication, all spirits have side effects that give them away. Be alert if for no other reason than you have become sick to your stomach in one's presence. It is entirely possible to see another entity in the eyes of one possessed as if another individual is looking at you through their eyes which indeed it is.

Another test is this: does that person have peace and joy? Is he or she depressed and confused? Can they look at you when they are speaking? Frequently a demon possessed person cannot look at you. Many times, they will twist away from you and perhaps even cross the street to avoid eye contact.

In this era, discerning of spirits is more valuable than ever before, for demon possession will continue to escalate as time goes on (*Revelation 9:20*). Never fear this gift; God has given us power over all the power of the enemy (*Luke 10:19*). Elisha told the young man that there are more with us than there are with them (*2 Kings 6:16-17*).

We belong to Jesus and He will never let us down, so don't be afraid if the Holy Spirit tries to develop this gift in your life: it can save you so much.

Chapter 2

DECLARATION OF WAR

The moment you and I turned to Jesus Christ for salvation our souls became a battleground. We are captives set free from Satan's stronghold and he simply cannot tolerate such an act of liberation. He declares war on us. Where we expected things to go right from the time we were born again, suddenly we found ourselves in almost insurmountable circumstances.

The enemy shot arrows of fear and doubt into our minds, sent trouble into the home, misunderstanding between us and those we love the most. In short order we discovered that we had an enemy and he was bent upon our destruction by any means possible.

This, unfortunately, is where some turn back to the old life. After all, Satan didn't bother us then. But if we will walk with Christ, then we will be at peace to some degree or another. Satan will never leave us alone completely and either we will learn how to overcome him and walk in victory, or else we will live miserable, dejected lives.

It is a pattern in the Bible. As soon as Jesus himself was baptized in the Jordan River, He was thrust into the wilderness to be tested by Satan. As soon as Elijah received the double portion of the Holy Spirit, the sons of the prophets buffeted him. As soon as the children of Israel left Egypt, they were beset by trials. And after Paul the Apostle turned to Christ, he was thrown into all sorts of trials and temptations. (See *2 Corinthians 11:23-27*.)

The Apostle Paul was tested in ways that we will never be called upon to suffer. We are not alone because a vast number of saints were tried before us. Satan is never going to let us off easily. Testing, however, will drive us to prayer and to the Word and those things will assure that we will walk in victory.

The thing that Satan wanted is found in *Isaiah 14:12-14*.

How art thou fallen from heaven, O Lucifer, son of the morning! how art thou cut down to the ground, which didst weaken the nations! For thou hast said in thine heart, I will ascend into heaven, I will exalt my throne above the stars of God: I will sit also upon the mount of the congregation, in the sides of the north: I will ascend above the heights of the clouds; I will be like the most High.

Psalm 48:1 says *"Great is the Lord and greatly to be praised in the city of our God, in the mountain of his holiness."* In *Job 26:7*, it states, *"He stretcheth out the north over the empty place, and hangeth the earth upon nothing."* From these verses we understand that in the northern part of the heavens there is a great empty place and this is where the throne of God is as seen in both *Psalms* and *Isaiah*.

That the empty places are there is now borne out by both astronauts and scientists. A vast cavern lies in that area in the constellation of Orion. Photographs even show indescribable colors and wonders in that area of the heavens.

Satan was there once as the director of praise. A beautiful being who ultimately rebelled against God. His wisdom and beauty assured him that he could be like God. That he could exalt his throne above the throne of God. As God, he could cause the

19

world to bow down before him and worship him in adoration. More than anything else, he wanted to be worshiped. Cast as lighting out of heaven, he did not give up his dream of world dominion, but has pursued that dream to this very day. Because of his deception, most of the world lies in darkness and error where religion is concerned.

Remember, Satan does not care how religious one is as long as he does not turn to the real light, Jesus Christ. Carrying this thought a little further let us look at *2 Thessalonians 2:4* where it says, *"Who opposes and exalts himself above all that is called God, or that is worshipped; so that he as God sitteth in the temple of God, shewing himself that he is God."*

During the tribulation when Satan sets up his headquarters in Jerusalem and the temple has been rebuilt, he will position himself in the holy place proclaiming to the whole world that he is God and he will demand to be worshipped by all tongues and people. Can't you hear him laughing and shouting, "I made it after all? Here I am sitting in the temple of God as God and the entire world has to worship me. I really pulled it off after all."

His victory, of course, will be short-lived for the king of glory will come and avenge His chosen people, Israel. But for that period of time Satan will have a heyday. We saw in the book of Isaiah that he said, *"I will ascend into heaven, I will exalt my throne, I will sit also on the mount"*. Satan still promises things to his followers that he cannot possibly give them. He is still positive in his affirmations of self-glory.

Example: A young man confessed his acts of homosexuality and prostitution, and myself and another friend joined hands and prayed. His eyes looked weary and he fell off his chair. We recognized demonic activity immediately and commanded them to leave him.

What we didn't know was that he had asked Satan to enter him and control his life. He wasn't looking for deliverance, as he liked his present life-style too much. Filth flowed from his lips during the next four hours and it was too hard to hold him down as he was taken over by forces stronger than we two women were. We called two other people to no avail as he literally kicked the kitchen apart.

During the four hours that followed, Satan spoke through him saying "I will give you power. I will give you wealth." Satan was promising this man all of the things that people want most in this life to refrain from being delivered from the spirits that now possessed him. Satan used the same phraseology "I will, I will, I will."

Children in the neighborhood heard the man's screams and a young girl of about fourteen years old motioned to me to come outside. She asked me if I had a cross and asked me to let her have it. I wanted to know why. The girl replied that she was a witch and knew how to handle demons. The girl said, "I can use the cross for protection, and then make the demons come into me. Since I know how to handle them, I can make them leave."

The very idea was so absurd that I shuddered to think that a young girl could handle demons. It did not take place, but it does show how Satan is deceiving the youth of today by alluring them into occult circles making them believe that they have power over them (demons). The only power over Satan and his works comes through the Holy Spirit and enters the life that is committed to Christ. The episode with the young man came to an end, but he was still possessed by evil spirits—but by choice, and continued his present life-style.

As long as we wear these robes of flesh, Satan will try various means of trying to destroy the Christian. Sometimes he tries to push them back in their walk with the Lord. If that fails, he tries to push them over the edge into error. He really doesn't care which method works and most of the time he just tries to make the believer's life miserable. He growls, threatens, and lunges, but remember he is on a leash and God holds the leash. He can come so far and no farther. He uses methods of fear, doubt, and unbelief to name a few. He will attack when our defenses are down or we are weak in our bodies. He will do his utmost to wear out the child of God.

Excerpts from A. W. Tozer: "A true Christian is a former slave who has escaped the galley and Satan cannot forgive him for this afront. A praying Christian is a constant threat to the stability of Satan's government. The Christian is a rebel loose in the world with access to the throne of God. Satan never knows from what direction the danger will come.

"The new Christian must be destroyed early or at least have his growth stunted so that he will be no real problem later on. The devil's master strategy for us Christians, then, is not to kill us physically, but to destroy our power to wage spiritual warfare. If Satan opposes the new Christian, he opposes still more bitterly the Christian who is pressing on toward a higher life in Christ.

"The spirit-filled life is not, as many suppose, a life of peace and quiet pleasure. Viewed one way is a pilgrim through a robber-infested forest. Viewed another way is grim warfare with the devil. Compromise will take the pressure off.

"Satan will not bother a Christian who has quit fighting. But the cost of quitting will be a life of peaceful stagnation. We sons of eternity simply cannot afford such a thing. The soul does indeed pass through dark nights of the soul, but our victory is assured through the Lord Jesus Christ.

"Never doubt in the dark what God showed you in the light, this is well worth remembering. No matter how powerful the attacks of the enemy, our great high priest will be there beside us because He has promised to never leave us or forsake us, *Hebrews 13*. Sometimes the conflicts are so great that the best one can do is whisper Jesus and when that name is spoken all heaven hears and the results are swift and immediate. Satan hates and fears that name exceedingly."

We live in the end times before Jesus comes back again. Today one can go to the corner store and purchase books on the occult, soul travel, channeling, horoscopes and how to cast spells. There has never been a time the attacks of Satan have been so malignant and filled with hatred. He knows his time is short and if he is going to back us up it must be now. Peter said, *"Beloved, think it not strange concerning the fiery trial which is to try you, as though some strange thing happened unto you"* (1 Peter 4:12).

Sometimes spirits come in families. A classic example is found in *1 Samuel 18*. The first spirit to attack King Saul was anger when David was extolled above him as he was ascribed to having slain ten thousand to Saul's one thousand. Anger gave way to envy and he began to watch David from then on. The next was a religious spirit that came upon Saul and he prophesied.

The Scriptures state clearly that this was an evil spirit. In verse 1 of the same chapter a spirit of murder came upon Saul and he tried to kill David. Next carne fear because the Lord was with David, but had departed from Saul. This is also true of those today who have evil spirits. The problem may have started with something that seemed innocent, say covetousness, but instead of letting it go that spirit was nourished and petted. This led to hatred and hatred to bitterness and bitterness to murder. If the chief spirit in an individual is lust, then other spirits can easily be perversion, uncleanness, homosexuality, hate and rebellion.

Example: A sixteen-year-old boy had serious problems. I looked into his eyes. They were too bright, too blue and the pupils were too small. The spirits were triggered when the power of the Holy Spirit came upon him and he fell backwards screaming. Myself and the pastor, plus six other men could not hold him down. His strength was so great he kicked a leg off of a piano and tore up the carpet he was lying on and I thought that he had been delivered that night. I saw him weeks later and he didn't want to look at me. What happened? His eyes looked the same. Had the door into the soulish area been opened? Had he really been delivered and let the demons back in again? Only the Lord knows the answers to these questions.

But one thing is become abundantly clear, if Christians are going to be in ministry, sooner or later they will probably encounter cases like this and they must be ready to deal with them. We are in a war. The Christian life is serious business. These things cannot be taken lightly. We can't fight alone; we must know the power of the Holy Spirit for He alone is capable of fighting against the powers of darkness. Being sensitive to the Holy Spirit is vitally important. Sensitivity comes through spending time with God, hearing His voice, and learning His ways. As one becomes sensitive to Him, he will sense many

24

things many times that no one else seems to detect. For instance, there are times when the enemy tightly binds a church service. Yet no one realizes what is wrong, except the one who has become sensitive to the Spirit of God, and that person will do battle with the enemy to loose the service. Indeed, there are those who are so insensitive to a bound service that they are not even aware that it is bound.

Some people are so sensitive to alien spirits when they travel that they take their own pillow because they can tell what spirit was there before them. This may seem radical, but it's true. I have had this experience resulting in jumbled and confused thoughts, half-formed dreams troubled me and I awoke in deep depression. I realized then that someone had slept on the pillow who was deeply confused, possibly even a mental case. When I switched pillows there was no further trouble.

When we become sensitive to the Holy Spirit it only follows that we become sensitive to all spirits. And though this can be a trial, it is necessary if we will be used of God. When I stay in a motel, I plead the blood of Jesus over the entire place and take my own pillow. The spirit world is more real than the one we live in and see every single day. If our eyes should be opened to what is around us at times, we would not be able to bear it. Yet there is never a need to fear, for if God should open our eyes to behold the enemy arrayed against us, He would also show us a heavenly host of angels sent to protect us. As Elisha, the man of God, told his servant, in *2 Kings 6:16-17*,

> *Fear not: for they that be with us are more than they that be with them. And Elisha prayed, and said, Lord, I pray thee, open his eyes, that he may see. And the Lord opened the eyes of the young man; and he saw: and*

behold, the mountain was full of horses and chariots of fire round about Elisha.

God is our protection, we belong to Him, and He will never let us down. He will be there in every battle we have to fight to keep us, to empower, and to see us safely through the day.

He loves us far beyond our ability to comprehend and has set Himself for our defense. Fear has no place in the heart or the mind of the child of God. We must face the enemy either in our own battles or for someone else and He is going to be there. We never have to fight by ourselves. Every time we tear down a stronghold of Satan His power is at our disposal. *"Behold, I give unto you power to tread on serpents and scorpions, and over all the power of the enemy: and nothing shall by any means hurt you"* *(Luke 10:19).*

He will never allow Satan to overtake us as we walk with Him and trust Him. *"And the Lord shall deliver me from every evil work, and will preserve me unto his heavenly kingdom: to whom be glory forever and ever. Amen"* *(2 Timothy 4:18).*

Chapter 3

CURSES, ARE THEY REAL?

David thought so, for in the *Psalms* we read,

As he loved cursing, so let it come unto him: as he delighted not in blessing, so let it be far from him. As he clothed himself with cursing as with his garment, so let it come into his inward parts like water, and like oil into his bones. Let it be unto him as the garment which covers him, and for a girdle wherewith he is girded continually. Let this be the reward of my adversaries from the Lord, and of them that speak evil against my soul. (Psalm 109:17-20).

The Living Bible is much stronger and more emphatic and reads in *verses 19-20, "Now may those curses return and cling to him like his clothing or his belt. This is the Lord's punishment upon my enemies who tell lies about me and threaten me with death."*

While attending my church, a prayer request was put in for a lady who had a bad hip and thought a curse had been put on her because the hip problem had been passed down for generations. King David believed that they could.

Another experience: My friend June asked me to write a book about a healing she had experienced and when the book was finished, we both agreed it was good and made plans for its publication. Then June called me and told me that another person's name was to be added to the book and I was shocked because the Holy Spirit had not anointed her.

June and her husband were mad, and accused me of all sorts of things including having spent the money they had given me to write the book, but the money was in the bank. June called myself and my daughter and another friend telling them that the Lord had shown her that I was going to be in a horrible car accident. I thought these were idle words, but I was involved in an accident with my motorcycle and in another accident while lying down in a van on a bed. Three weeks later my car was totaled—three accidents in three weeks, but I was undamaged.

What was going on? Then I was on the road again in Idaho and got shot in a freak accident and wound up in a hospital, but I was okay. What's wrong with me? Is there sin in my life? What was happening? I had no idea! Back home I asked the Lord, "What is going on?" His reply was, "June has put a curse on you."

I was dazed and surprised that a fellow Christian would do that to me. Suddenly it all made sense. I searched the scriptures and *2 Corinthians 10:4* assured me that the weapons of my *armor "were not carnal, but mighty through God to the pulling down strongholds."* *Luke 10:19* told me that God had delegated his power to me so that I could fearlessly face the enemy.

What was it that David had said in *Psalm 109:17-20*? Yes,
As he loved cursing, and it came back upon him: as he delighted not in blessing, so let it be far from him. As he clothed himself with cursing like as with his garment, so let it seep into his inward (life) like water, and like oil into his bones. Let it be to him as the raiment with which he covers himself, and for the girdle with which he is girded continually. Let this be the reward of my adversaries

28

from the Lord, and of those who speak evil against my life.
May those curses return and cling to him like his garment or his belt,

I felt that this was the answer and I was on scriptural ground. First of all, I nullified the curse to make it of no more effect and then I began to send the words back to June that she had spoken. You are not putting a curse on the sender, in this case June, because you are returning to them something that belongs to them.

You are never to accept words spoken against you anymore than you would accept a package left at your door addressed to someone else, you would send it back. The words do not belong to you, they belong to the person who sent them. And upon that basis you refuse them and send them back. It wasn't easy and release didn't come immediately; but it did come. And the strange incidents did come to an end soon as she figured out what she was fighting.

Sometimes an individual may have a curse put upon them and suffer endlessly because they don't know what it is they are fighting. As soon as light comes into the problem victory is assured. Please understand, curses are sometimes idly spoken and people don't mean them as a curse, but the effects can be just as deadly. Whether or not June had deliberately put a curse on my life, we don't know, but she was purposeful in her intentions because she did call three people to proclaim the evil tidings.

David wrote these awesome words in *Psalm 64:2-8,*

Hide me from the secret counsel of the wicked; from the insurrection of the workers of iniquity: Who whet their tongue like a sword, and bend their bows to shoot their arrows, even bitter words: That they may shoot in secret at the perfect: suddenly do they shoot at him, and fear not. They encourage themselves in an evil matter: they commune of laying snares privily; they say, Who shall see them? They search out iniquities; they accomplish a diligent search: both the inward thought of every one of them, and the heart, is deep. But God shall shoot at them with an arrow; suddenly shall they be wounded. So they shall make their own tongue to fall upon themselves: all that see them shall flee away.

God is ultimately the avenger. Later, I drove by June's church and the building was closed to services. June's husband had been having an affair and they got a divorce and the whole church emptied out. One cannot get by with putting curses on another: in the end they are the ones who will lose everything. Their words will come back upon them. Misunderstandings do arise among Christians, but these are to be dealt with as mature people, threats and curses do not belong in Christian relationships.

An evangelist was staying in the home of my pastor and their daughter was pregnant at thirty-six and the evangelist was concerned because their daughter's baby might be born with Down syndrome at her age. The pastor immediately came against the words and rebuked the power of such words and dispelled the fear and the baby was born normal.

Curses are for real and if we allow them to attach themselves to us, it will be to our undoing. We must see them for what they are and return the words to the sender for they do not belong to you. Don't take them lightly.

A young man did something quite innocently and made a lady angry and she called the words after him, "I curse you; I curse you; you are going to die!" The youth laughed at her words. But curses are not a laughing matter. They are to be dealt with as soon as the one upon whom the curse has been placed recognizes it. The Bible says life and death are in the power of the tongue, *Proverbs 18:21.*

Kahuna Curses: In Hawaii there are white and black Kahuna. The white Kahuna, of course, works white magic; that is, they put spells on people that bring blessing that are more or less harmless. The black Kahuna work black magic. They do incantations and place curses on lives that can be extremely vicious.

I wanted to know how they do this. The minster's wife said if a person wants something bad to happen to someone that they have a grudge against, then that person will obtain a bit of their enemy's clothing, even a fragment of a finger nail or a piece of hair will do. Perspiration or urine can also be used, but these are, of course, harder to get. Whatever it is that they obtain is taken to the Kahuna and he uses it somehow to put a curse on the individual. Do the curses actually work? "Yes," she replied and we are watching one now very closely.

A young Hawaiian girl took it into her head that she was in love with a married serviceman and he did not respond to her advances. Somehow, she managed to get a bit of his clothing and took it to a Black Kahuna priest. He put a spell on the soldier that was intended to make him leave his family and fall in love with the young girl. It worked; it wasn't long before he left his family and moved in with the girl.

Christians can have curses put on them. Yes, my husband and I have witnessed it and we were watching this situation because the soldier was still with the girl, but there was a five-year time limit on the curse. We were not around after the five years was up so we didn't know if the man reunited with his family.

31

Christians say this is impossible. It cannot happen. But does being a Christian automatically mean they are exempt from such things?

Illness from curses: A friend entered a prayer request for a lady who had a bad hip and thought a curse had been put on her because the hip problem had been passed down from generation to generation. I firmly believed at that time that curses could not be put on Christians. Again, we must remind ourselves that David, the Psalmist, believed otherwise.

When I had all those accidents that occurred in a short period of time, I had wrongly assumed that June had only spoken idle words and that she would back her words with powerful intent was incredulous. I was dumbfounded, but it all made sense.

I knew nothing about undoing curses. *2 Corinthians 10:4* assured me that the weapons of my warfare were not carnal; that is, they were not of a physical nature, so that meant they had to be spiritual. *Luke 10:19* told me that God had delegated to me His mighty power over the enemy so that I could fearlessly face Satan and his works. But wait! What was it David had said in the 109th Psalm, *"May those curses return and cling to him like his garment or his belt."* I felt this was the answer and now I am on scriptural ground.

First of all, I nullified the curse in Jesus' name to make it without effect and then I began sending the words that June had spoken back to her. Wouldn't that be putting a curse back on her? An emphatic no! You are not cursing them; you are simply returning to them what is theirs. Never accept words spoken against you anymore than you would accept a package left at your door that was not yours. The words do not belong to you, they belong to the one who spoke them. Upon that basis you do what David did—you send them back. As I steadfastly stood against the curse and returned the words to the sender, the mysterious accidents came to an end.

Sometimes a person suffers endlessly from a curse spoken at them because they do not know what they are fighting. But as soon as light comes into the problem victory is assured.

We must understand that sometimes curses are idly spoken and people don't mean them as a curse, but the effects, however, can be just as deadly for words are extremely powerful. Whether or not June had deliberately put a curse on my life we will probably never know, but she was purposeful in her intentions because, as written above, she did call three people to proclaim the evil tidings.

Hidden in God: "So they shall make their own tongue to fall upon themselves: all that see them shall flee away" (Psalm 64:8). Did you really hear those last words; they shall make their tongues to fill upon themselves. You see God ultimately avenges.

My son Stephen: I was in bed seven months while I carried him. His crib was in our bedroom because the house was small. One day I was sitting on the bed and I felt a black terrifying presence enter the room. With its entrance Stephen began to scream and for a long, suspended moment of time I did not move and when the presence gradually receded, I went to the crib and was stunned to see the beautiful blue eyes changed to yellowish green eyes. I knew nothing about spirits or spiritual warfare, but I did know that an alien force had seized control of my son. For three long years he screamed day and night and the pastor offered no hope, but said that the God would not allow a child to be possessed.

The result was that Stephen's life was a variable merry-go-round of horror stories. Through the course of his life, he would be thrown from foster home to psychiatric hospital, to State mental institution, to correctional facilities and to prison, not once, but over and over again. If he were placed in a foster home the workers would suffer a nervous breakdown as I did. He was incorrigible and was expelled from both the first and second grades because the teachers could not control him.

At age twelve a visiting minister asked to see his picture and asked who had laid hands on this child. My husband and I replied no one. He went on to describe a lady in white, dark and swarthy and she had come from a foreign country and that she had taken him into a back room and laid hands on him and placed a curse on his life. Both of us reacted at the same moment. Of course!

When Stephen was three months old, we had gone to El Charro's to eat. A tall dark woman, a waitress dressed in white, took Stephen from my arms and disappeared with him. I remember being frantic and wanted Bob to go get him, but Bob told me that I was worrying needlessly and assured me that this woman was just showing Stephen off to the kitchen help. Our minister friend nodded that she is the one all right, and all that had happened to this child was because of that curse. Stephen is free today and the wild animal look is gone from his eyes and they are blue again.

Curses are indeed real and we must recognize them for what they are and refuse them. They can cause physical ailments, oppression, and depression; they can limit one's ability to pray effectively, or even read the Word. Never take them lightly, they are serious indeed.

Chapter 4

SOUL TIES

What is a soul tie? A soul tie is an unnatural affection that binds two people together. It is a relationship that exists beyond the normal level of affection and does not have to be called "love". It is what the scriptures call inordinate. *Colossians 3:5, "Mortify therefore your members which are upon the earth; fornication, uncleanness, inordinate affection, evil concupiscence, and covetousness, which is idolatry."*

A soul tie does not mean that the two people are involved in a homosexual relationship. Indeed, soul ties need not even have anything to do with sex, but certainly can lead to that. Soul ties at best are unhealthy and at worst deadly. They bind one individual to another so that the two persons involved begin to feel that they cannot be apart. And the thought of permanent separation brings a sense of suffering and loss too great to contemplate.

Soul ties are spiritual bonds that tie one spirit to another. Individuals will do anything and go anywhere to be with the other person. Soul ties can develop between women, especially spiritual women. They can develop between a man and a woman or even between children and their parents. That soul ties are deadly in the extreme is a fact. They should be broken at all costs and be avoided as one should avoid drinking a cup of coffee laced with arsenic. Ultimately, they can only bring harm to the spiritual side of man, bondage to another person, and unutterable suffering.

Example: Linda's baby, Mark, had ear problems and she held him a lot as a small child and a soul tie was developed because of holding him so much while he was sick for so long, although Linda had no idea. Mark cried for hours at school as a result of his separation from Linda and Linda moped around home suffering, feeling lost and confused while waiting for school to get out. Mother and son wept through their days, waiting to be together.

Linda realized the situation was not good but didn't know what was wrong until an evangelist recognized the problem, and prayer and the power of the Holy Spirit was made on behalf of Linda and Mark and the soul tie was broken. Linda was aware of her newfound freedom and Mark went off to school happy. He had previously been making poor grades and was soon getting A's. The entire problem was resolved when recognized for what it was and its power broken in prayer.

However, it is not always that easy. A soul tie can be desirable, sweet and alluring. The closeness one experiences with another individual is not in itself offensive, it's desirable, it feels good, it even feels right. So, to think of giving up that relationship doesn't even enter the mind unless one is forced to face up to the facts.

Soul ties are not of God, they are unhealthy. They rob one's sense of values; they can destroy homes; they can tear down one's own spiritual relationship with the Lord. For in a soul tie individuals want to be with their counterpart even more so than they want to be with their own families, or even with God.

Soul ties can impair judgment as to what is right or wrong. The bondage between two such souls can become so strong that they will all but abandon spouses and children to be with and please the partner of such a relationship. Soul ties, though not apparent

36

in the beginning, lead only to bondage and oppression. In spite of the seeming sweetness of such a relationship, in the end an oppressively heavy spirit will be present. To tear a soul tie apart causes such grief, as one person put it, death would have been sweeter.

Example: Amy, a young lady, was involved in a soul tie relationship that got out of hand and had wound up in sexual perversion. She was going through intense suffering. They were like one person so keen was their love. Amy came to the Lord and was gripped with conviction over this abnormal friendship, and her friend broke off their relationship to find a new partner.

Amy's suffering was real, her spirit was being torn from the spirit of the other girl and the process was terrible. Now, not all homosexuals have soul ties although their lifestyle is contrary to scripture and their love unhealthy. There are those like Amy who simply start off being drawn to each other in a soul tie relationship, a bond that resulted in a sexual alliance. This is the reason that the break up between some gay partners causes such pain.

Example: Two Christian ladies, Leah (her husband was the minister of a very large church) and Beth. Both women had a deep walk with the Lord. And it was this very depth of spirit that drew them together. They literally soared in the spirit together and before either of them realized what was happening in their friendship, a soul tie had formed between them. Now being together took on a new meaning. They made excuses to be together.

They were spending an excessive amount of time together; they understood each other, long hours lingering over a lunch or praying together. It was wrong because they were putting each other first even before their families and God.

It was wrong because it was a soul tie. When they were apart, they were miserable. If one called the other, one would leave their children and husband to fend for themselves. There was only one thing that mattered—that they were together to the exclusion of everyone else. There was never a wrong word or touch between them, yet it was wrong.

The sweetness they had known before in their friendship began to disappear and was replaced with heaviness, an indescribable oppression. When they were together, they were complete, one. But when they were forced to separate, it was like a living death.

Beth likened their relationship to two pieces of spaghetti that were hopelessly wound around each other. They could only be separated by being tom apart and such an idea was unthinkable. It was Leah's husband who finally took charge of the situation as he had stayed on the sidelines watching. He called and asked Beth to come to the church where Leah was present also. He confronted them, thinking the relationship had turned into a sexual bondage, and demanded that they come clean.

Regarding homosexuals: Certainly not all homosexuals have soul ties though their lifestyle is contrary to scripture and their love unhealthy. There are those, however, who like Beth and Leah started out as simply being drawn to one another in a soul tie relationship. A bond formed and grew into a sexual alliance. This is the reason some suffer so terribly in the breakup of a gay relationship. It was a wonderful, delightful relationship. They put each other first to the exclusion of everyone else, even their family as well as God. It was wrong because it was a soul tie.

The sweetness that was there in the beginning was replaced with heaviness, a terrible oppression. They said a tearful goodbye. They did break the soul tie through prayer that was the rending asunder of two souls that had become one. And the suffering was nearly unbearable. In time, these women recovered and returned to happy normal lives. As of this time, Leah went home to be with the Lord and Beth guards herself to avoid such a relationship of ever developing again.

Soulish Music: We are body, soul and spirit. The spirit is that part of us that lives forever. The spirit is also the part of us that worships God and responds to the overtures of the Holy Spirit. Our spirit-man focuses on heaven and those things that are eternal. Our soulish area focuses on the pleasure things offer.

Perhaps you have heard someone mention that a lot of our contemporary music in church today is soulish. That is, it makes us feel good, and so we respond by clapping or dancing, but that type of music fails to touch the spirit. It does not turn our hearts to God but to the fleshly part of us. That is what a soul tie does. It appeals to our fleshy side, our carnal side. It stirs the emotions but leaves the spirit vulnerable & untouchable.

Karen lived in Colorado and her twin died at birth and in some bizarre way her parents blamed Karen for the death. As in so many cases when parents reject children, they try sundry methods of gaining their parent's attention and affection.

In Karen's case she showered her parents with gifts and lived by them even as an adult. But her gifts were rejected and her attention spumed. It seemed that the harder she tried the more they rejected her. Yet in spite of the apparent rejection, a soul tie does exist between Karen and her parents.

At one time Karen tried to escape this bondage by moving to another state to work, but almost immediately that soulish tie brought her home again. If she left town to visit a friend, she was compelled to stop on the outskirts of town to purchase cards to send back to her parents, even if she was gone for only the weekend. After she reached the home of her friend, she instantly called her parents. This from a woman in her late thirties. Karen had been urged to leave the small town and make a life for herself, but this seemed too great of a sacrifice. She was virtually a prisoner to her family. This was both sad and unnecessary, for Jesus came to open prison doors and set us free.

David and Jonathan: It is impossible to read the Old Testament without seeing the soul tie that existed between these men. In *1 Samuel 18:1* we read, *"And it came to pass that when he had made an end of speaking unto Saul, that the soul of Jonathan was knit with the soul of David, and Jonathan loved him as his own soul."*

When Jonathan was slain in battle David was overcome with grief and cried out, *"I am distressed for you, my brother Jonathan: very pleasant have you been unto me: your love to me was wonderful, passing the love of women"* (2 Samuel 18:26).

Was this love approved by the Lord, apparently so, but why? For by their own admission, it was a soul tie. But you see, the men always put God first. They could live normal lives apart from one another. They never allowed it to become a consuming relationship to the exclusion of everyone else. God continued to guide their lives on an individual basis. They did not have to be together. When they were together, their attention was centered upon God, not upon each other.

The gay society loves this particular portion of scripture and uses it to defend and exonerate their lifestyle. They take the phrase *"thy love was wonderful to me, surpassing the love of women"* and claim that David and Jonathan were involved in a homosexual relationship, but this is nowhere indicated in

40

scripture. Rather, the two men enjoyed a deep love that exceeded physical love and was guided and controlled by the Holy Spirit.

All too often, however, the Spirit is left out and two souls gravitate to one another in an unholy alliance that soon becomes either perversion or at least out-of-the-ordinary as the Bible states. Thus, a soul tie is destructive and must at all costs be broken. The focal point in any relationship, if it is to be wholesome, must be centered in Jesus Christ.

Kindred Spirits: Kindred spirits are not soul ties for they are centered in the spirit rather than the soul. We have all at some time encountered another Christian with whom we have an instantaneous rapport though we have never met before. It seems that we had always known them.

Among Christians who have a deep walk with the Lord and understanding of spiritual values, this is a more or less common occurrence. I attended a church and the minister's wife spoke and we had eye contact and instantly we knew each other. In one blinding flash I knew her, not that I knew anything about her, but I recognized her spirit and the same with her towards me. After the service we met by unspoken consent and embraced. We knew each other by the spirit for we had like spirits. We never had to be together or rarely had lunch or even talked on the telephone, but when we did, there was perfect understanding and Christ-centered fellowship. In such a case a soul tie never forms.

Madame Guyan and Father LaCombe: Madame Guyan wrote in her autobiography as soon as she saw LaCombe she was surprised to feel an interior grace which "I now call communication such as I had never experienced with any person. It seemed to me that an influence of grace came from him to me through the innermost of the soul return from me to him in such a way that he felt the same effect. This is a pure and holy union in which God alone operates."

Fellowship in the Spirit: Does the fellowship enjoyed by kindred spirits brings heaviness or oppression? Such fellowship never brings bondage. Kindred spirits never have to be together in order to satisfy that soulish part of them. If such a relationship is dissolved, it never feels like a part of one's soul is being ripped and torn apart. They are utterly content to make contact only now and then. The love that exits between those of kindred spirits is pure and holy and all together right before God. In a soul tie relationship, the two involved will always try and justify being together, especially if the soul tie leads to sexual perversion.

Does not the Bible say that to the pure all things are pure and are they not pure if they are children of God? I met a lady who was involved in more than one soul tie both with men and women. In each instance there was a sexual encounter.

She justifies this by saying that it's an "expression of God's love". But God's love does not operate on a soulish level, it operates on a spiritual level and soul ties are soulish.

What to be aware of: When a person has a compelling urge to be with another individual with a variable gravitation to another soul, that is the first indication that a soul tie is being established. After a soul tie has been initiated, there will be demands on one another's time including the exclusion of everyone else, even one's own family. The sweetness one experiences in the beginning of such a relationship will eventually dissolve and a brooding depression will begin, especially when the two are forced to be apart.

Unless the soul tie is immediately broken, the two people will find their souls so intertwined the thought of separation and the dissolution of such a relationship will bring unutterable suffering and pain.

The very love in a soul tie is in itself a form of perversion and should be avoid at all cost. In the end, it can lead only to oppressiveness of spirit and extreme bondage. Their spiritual life will suffer and the love of the other individual will eventually overshadow their love for Christ.

To be willing for the soul tie to be broken makes the severance much easier. To recognize it for what it is and give it over to God is the answer. He alone can break the bondage and He will always deal with it through prayer. This is the only way soul ties can be taken care of. "I know before God that this is a soul tie and in the Name of Jesus Christ, I break it and declare that it comes to nothing. I command an undoing of all-unnatural ties and freedom in Jesus' Name."

Chapter 5

PSYCHIC PRAYER

It bypasses God: Physic prayer is prayer that bypasses both Father and Son and is directed toward the individual in question. It can be used for harmful intent. It can also be used quite innocently.

The Word assures us that when we pray in the name of Jesus, God will grant us our petition providing that our petition lies within the will of God for us. But with psychic prayer the one praying sees an image of the person for whom he is praying in his mind, and he is praying toward that, and not for that person. In reality he is praying to the face he envisions in his mind.

Mysterious Afflictions: The one who is the recipient of that prayer may undergo one or more mysterious afflictions. The most severe will be acute debilitating physical weakness. A weakness that leaves the doctors completely stymied. A black cloud of depression or oppression settles upon the individual to whom the psychic prayer is intended. Oppression is heavier than depression. There will be an inability to think clearly and there will be a "tight band" around the head at times. It will be difficult to function in everyday life and there may be a desire to hide in bed and never face the world again. If a person experience several of the above symptoms at the same time, for a prolonged period of time, chances are they are the subject of psychic attack.

Who uses psychic power? Ordinarily it is someone with a vendetta against another person. Some even delude themselves into believing that they are actually doing the other person a service by such praying.

I had been in a church where they were told to pray that an individual would not be able to eat or sleep until they received salvation. Pray they will be miserable until they find the Lord. I realized in retrospect that such praying was far from being in the will of God: it was in fact psychic prayer. The conviction of the Holy Spirit is gentle, not harassing and tormenting.

Does God answer such praying? The answer is an emphatic no! Because the person praying is not praying to God; he is praying to the image of the one he sees in his mind. The effects of that prayer, however, are far-reaching, for words cross distance in the same way true prayer does.

The person praying watches for the answer in the life of the one he is praying against (not for) and he sees his words take hold. He thinks God is answering his prayer, but this is not true for that prayer was not channeled through the Father in the name of Jesus. Oh, in lip service perhaps, but the truth is the prayer went straight to the image he saw in his mind. I was told that in the Bishop Museum in Hawaii is the image of a black kahuna priest who personally prayed to death fifty people. Psychic power and psychic prayer are potent indeed and one should never underestimate the effects they can have upon others.

Vera: Vera left her rather staid denominational church for a Pentecostal church. There she received the baptism in the Holy Spirit and her life was transformed. The people in her old church began to pray against her, feeling that she had stumbled into error. The prayers probably went something like this "Lord, deal severely in Vera's life until she returns to us and make her miserable and dissatisfied where she is. Show her that she is wrong."

Whatever they prayed the words were not correctly channeled through the Father in Jesus' name, for Vera came under extreme psychic attack. She felt thickheaded and her thoughts were scattered and confused. Heavy oppression seized her and she began staying more and more to herself. Such weakness gripped her body that she could no longer do those things that once brought her pleasure.

I was staying in her home and saw her dilemma. As soon as Vera began sharing with me, I knew what was happening to her. Vera began to resist the psychic prayers in the name of Jesus and soon regained her old vitality. She had been aware of the fact that her old friends were praying against her, but had not realized the power those prayers conveyed.

Rev. Charles: Rev. Charles was a radio and TV minister who has for years enjoyed a wide ministry. Suddenly he was struck down by a mysterious physical weakness. At the same time a strange lethargy seized him and he nearly succumbed to the dark oppression that hovered about him. By his admission he wanted to go to bed and pull up the covers over his head and never get up again. A lady who did some taping for him recognized the signs and went to bat for him. She shared with him what the problem was and he began fighting against it himself. It vanished almost at once.

"I am sending you my love." People say that all the time meaning that while they are absent from someone, they are still thinking of them in living terms. By the same token, people can

send hate, vengeance, retaliation and real harm to another person in the psychic realm. It is altogether possible for someone to send his or her presence to another individual. That presence may seem indescribably sweet and alluring or it can be harmful and fearful.

I once held meetings for a pastor in my area. The Pastor's wife told me that she had had an out-of-body experience and that she and her husband had once operated a mind power clinic when they pastored in another state.

The knowledge of the clinic was so secretive that no one in their church was even aware of its existence. She also said that some believed in some mysterious "neutral power" that one could tap into and use for either good or evil. This could only be psychic power. I later learned that other ministers today believe in the "neutral power" too and say that if you learn certain secret techniques that you can perform miracles.

Strange things began occurring in my home once the meeting came to a close. There would be an oppressive spiritual darkness hovering within and I would sense the presence of the minister.

Animals are often aware of such phenomena and will react. My dog would suddenly stand erect and stare at the invisible forms of the minister and his wife. She would sniff upward at the taller form of the woman, then turn her attention to the shorter form of the pastor. This happened regularly for about two weeks before I told the minister's wife what was happening. I also told her that I knew exactly who it was and it never happened again.

"You can't leave my church": I have had people contact me for help because they have wanted to leave the church that they were in, but could not because of the psychic power holding them there. They felt like prisoners. A few people did leave, but were

soon drawn back almost immediately. As much as they desired to seek out another church, they could not.

Two women that I knew left a church. They had attended it for several years but they hated not only the bondage, but they felt error proclaimed from the pulpit. They both left, one of them a single lady and the other a wife and mother. All of them came under severe psychic oppression accompanied by headaches and physical weakness.

It was a difficult time for all of them. It seemed almost impossible to function or to think, even though loving, caring Christians surrounded them. The pastor of the church they had previously attended was alarmed and angry at their departure. So, he began praying against them trying, perhaps innocently, to draw them back again. When the two families began fighting against psychic power and psychic prayer, the battle came to an end. In fact, the church they had left collapsed and the pastor moved to another city.

Rev. Martin was another pastor who attempted to keep too tight of a control on the people. He sought to gain control over their lives. He told a young woman whose husband was, at that time, in Vietnam that if she didn't come to church every time the doors were open that her husband would be killed, and he was!

The pastor told another woman, a young mother, that if she wasn't in every service that her child would die, and the baby did die. Words, words, words they can be used for good or they can be used for evil. And words, like prayer, can be psychic, spanning the distance between two people to bring harm.

No crystal ball: Psychic power drums up the image of swarthy skinned women with a scarf over their head peering into the murky depths of a crystal ball. But psychic power can be used by ordinary

48

people and, as we have already seen, by ordinary Christians. Misdirected prayer is words spoken to harm in some way and is an instrument of Satan. Psychic prayer should never pass the lips of one who professes to live for Christ.

Brotherhood of the Rose: This was a movie shown on TV years ago. It involved two brothers who several times each day were forced to repeat key phrases given to them by their mother. As a result of such brain-washing, they came completely under their mother's control. They were compelled to obey everything she said and that included murder.

Many ministers today command their flocks to repeat certain phrases after them. If the response of the congregation is mild, he will shout, "I can't hear you!" This will continue until the words of the pastor are being screamed back at him. He calls this "getting it into your spirit" but in reality, it's a form of control. This, of course, is not entirely bad, but it's true that some pastors do this repeatedly to bring the people under their control. When that happens, it becomes psychic power.

The first time I taught on this subject, a 16-year-old boy was passing by the church and he said that the Holy Spirit drew him inside. The message opened his eyes to the oppression he was suffering and he was totally released that night from psychic influences. I saw him again later and he was still free and serving the Lord.

Brother M: This minister came to Tucson to preach and stayed in our home. When he was present, there was a bond developing between us that I had never experienced before. It seemed like Madam Guyon and Father LaCombe who could communicate without talking.

All the time he was with us it was wonderful, but when he left to fly home, I would come under a terrible oppression. It would hang in the house for days until I could pray my way through it. The last time he was in our home, I awoke early and could feel his presence in our bedroom.

My husband was gone, as he had left for work early. It was not a good sensation, it was strong and it was evil, but it was Brother M's presence. Feeling vulnerable and powerfully drawn to him, I began to pray and refused the overtures he was making to me.

After my family moved to the city where his church was located, I had lunch with a lady from his congregation. She shared with me that Brother M had had a "thing" for her for a long time. But she also related some very disturbing news of which I had been unaware. It seems that a deceiving spirit had taken hold of Brother M some years before. He even had "spiritual wives" living in the church behind the baptistery.

Other women swore that when their husband had been out of town on business that Brother M would use astral projection and come into their homes and have sex with them. I was shocked, but I learned a valuable lesson too. The sweet beguiling relationship that I had enjoyed in the beginning was him trying to deceive me.

Any time one senses such closeness and sweetness with another human being that afterwards leaves them oppressed and confused, it is the Holy Spirit saying to be very careful, something is wrong and the sweetness is not what it appears to be.

If you are in ministry: I seriously doubt that anyone can be in ministry for very long before someone, somewhere, begins praying physic prayer against them. People get upset over trivial things and feel that the ministry is in need of correction so they take it upon themselves to pray against it.

I had no idea the first time it happened to me. I then would discover that there were people who would pray their will upon me and send their prayers directly toward me. I only knew that I had become too weak in my body to function in everyday life.

A tight band formed around my head and it was mud to think. The darkness of the spirit world had descended upon me, but how, why? I struggled against these unknown forces for three long weeks when someone put Watchman Nee's book, "The Latent Power of The Soul" into my hands. As I read it, I began to understand what was wrong was somebody was praying against me. Perhaps not intentionally meaning me harm, but the effects were the same nevertheless.

Their prayers were bypassing God the Father and God the Son and were being aimed directly at me. Watchman Nee told how he had been under just such an attack. Weakness had gripped his body until he was totally unable to function.

In answer to his prayers, God immediately sent a brother to him who understood exactly what was taking place. He had, in fact, gone through the same himself and had been bedfast for physical weakness. He explained psychic prayer to Nee and told him to cut himself off from all such prayer in Jesus' name. He did and it left almost at once.

This was a wonderful answer to me and I instantly began to pray the simple prayer "I cut myself off from all physic prayer in Jesus' name. My strength returned, my mind cleared the darkness, heaviness lifted and I was soon able to resume normal living. Since then, I have shared this truth with a number of people and the severance prayer in every instance accomplished victory. Please understand that you may have to pray that prayer more than once, especially if you have been under attack for a long period of time, but God is sure to answer it and set you free.

Praying correctly: Every one of us must be diligent in channeling our prayers through Jesus' name as the scriptures admonish us. And carefully avoid directing our prayers to some face we may be seeing in our minds, for psychic prayer is a form of witchcraft and must at all cost be avoided. The Psalmist said, *"Set a watch before my mouth; keep the door of my lips"* (Psalm 141:3).

Chapter 6

CAN CHRISTIANS
BE POSSESSED?

A great controversy: This is a topic that has been discussed and disagreed upon for years. Many say absolutely not, others are just as adamant in their belief that Christians can be possessed. So, to tackle this subject is sure to add more controversy.

People argue that since we are under the blood that we are safe from demonic activity. Besides, does the Bible not declare that two cannot walk together except they be in agreement? *(Amos 3:3).* However, there are still others who teach that if the Christian opens the door to a spirit, it can take residence. However, an evil spirit and the Holy Spirit do not walk together. They are in constant conflict; they are diametrically opposed to each other and are engaged in continual warfare. I can only tell you what I have encountered in my own ministry.

Larry's story: In one of my meetings, so many came to be prayed for that some were forced onto the platform to make room. I approached a young red-headed man barely out of his teens. I reached out to touch him and abruptly his right foot shot out and went straight through the wall. He drew back his fist to strike me, but missed and his hand also went through the wall. This was one of my first encounters with demonic activity and I began to take authority.

Three other ministers in the congregation quickly came forward to assist in his deliverance. There was no foaming at the mouth or vile odors as in same cases I had seen, but there were blood-chilling screams as the evil spirits left him. Larry was set free that night and the last I heard of him he was working in California.

Not choosy: Demon possession can occur in the lives of the poorest of the poor, or the most elite. Evil spirits want only one thing—a body to inhabit and live through.

Vickie was a very wealthy individual who lived in a luxurious home and enjoyed all the benefits that money affords. She was a devoted Christian. When her mother was in an accident, Vickie flew to an island known for its demonic activity to care for her. Her father was involved in the occult and the home was full of darkness and occult objects.

In some way, unknown to me, Vickie opened the door to the spirit world while she was there and three spirits stepped inside to make her body their home. When she returned home, she was filled with fear and torment. Occultic happenings began taking place around her. She began fasting and praying for her own deliverance and finally came to some evangelistic meetings.

On a Friday night she came forward for prayer and fell backwards to the floor screaming. Since it was impossible to take her into a side room where she could be dealt with privately, the spirits had to be tackled right where she lay.

Four people came forward to help with her deliverance, two men and two women. For the next fifteen minutes Vickie writhed, barked, hissed and screamed. The three spirits that had seized her were identified as fear, torment and witchcraft, and barking they came out one by one. Where did this lady trip up? I had no idea, but somewhere along the way she opened the door to these spirits. And whenever a door is opened the enemy happily walks inside.

I met Julie in British Columbia, an attractive dark-haired lady that owned an antique store. One night while praying for people, I came to this woman whom I had never met until that night. Julie collapsed on my shoulder sobbing and in the next instant she began to manifest an evil spirit. Her body began writhing as she cried out in agony.

This particular church had a deliverance team that was always ready for such cases and she was quickly taken into a side room to be dealt with. There, however, she rebelled and insisted on returning to the prayer line to be prayed for. Since I had no idea what was happening, I was surprised to see Julie standing before me again. When I began to pray, Julie reacted in the same manner as before, only this time she was completely out of control. She twisted and writhed and a scream tore from her lips. Now the deliverance team could not get her to a place of privacy, but were forced to deal with her where she was. Julie was set free, but she was confused and frightened.

The following morning, she called me and asked incredulously how could this happen? "I have been saved and filled with the spirit for years." Of course, I could not tell her when it happened although I found out later that Julie had been going with a married man and perhaps that was the open door needed for those spirits to enter. I explained to Julie that we are body, soul and spirit—a being.

A Christian's spirit can never be possessed because it has been bought with the blood of Jesus and is fully protected. But there are areas in the soul that can be open to Satan and when he takes control of those areas, the body is also affected.

Isaiah penned the words, *"the yoke shall be destroyed because of the anointing" (Isaiah 10:27)*, whether it comes through the laying on of hands or through some gift of the Spirit because the Holy Spirit and an alien spirit are incompatible, and that is why an evil spirit reacts to the anointing. Whereas, before that spirit may have lain dormant for years, it is suddenly triggered to activity by the true anointing of the Holy Spirit.

Carolyn was the mother of four children, but she was so bound by torment that in church she would hug her coat around her in an effort to hide. She cowered around other Christians, yet she herself loved the Lord.

All of her husband's begging and encouragement failed to bring relief to her tortured soul. She feared to leave the house and felt safe and comfortable only with her immediate family. If she was forced to be in her home alone, she was so riddled by fear that she would panic.

I first met Carolyn in a prayer line in British Columbia. When prayer was offered, she dropped to the floor and the deliverance team quickly got her into the side room to deal with her. The chief demon told the team that there were twenty-seven other demons in her body. Though she received some help that first night, they were a long way from setting her completely free. Night after night one or two would depart.

Watching the process was like watching a bud come into full flower. Her coat in which she "hid" was discarded and she began openly praising God, then she began to smile and her eyes lost the glazed, haunted look. In the course of her deliverance, they learned that when she was in college, she opened the door to demonic influences. She was involved in every type of perversion known to man, and as well had delved deeply into various kinds

56

of the occult. The spirits had entered at that time and had full intentions of making her body their habitation for her entire life, but today, by the grace of God, she is free and radiant.

Playing with Danger: People today play with all types of danger and believe them to be harmless. They discard the fact that Satan plays for keeps and is deadly serious. Teenagers think it's cool to listen to tapes like Black Sabbath and Vanilla Ice.

One boy began occupying himself with just such music. Soon a classic Christian youth was almost a monster—a monster who screamed obscenities at his mother and made life miserable for the entire family. The mother and father began doing warfare for their son. Today he is much better, but he still struggles against the influence of heavy metal music. Heavy metal music is an instrument of Satan. It makes inroads into the lives of our youth.

A teen-age revival was occurring in the Northwest. Kids came from everywhere to get in on this move of God. And though they were excited and thrilled with what the Lord was accomplishing in their lives, some of them began to experience deep personal struggles against inside forces. Some had to be delivered from satanic or occultic influences in their lives.

In the high school the teenagers attended there were three different satanic cults and the same teenagers had innocently delved into the spirit world. Activities such as tarot cards, seances, black and white magic and other types of the occult are the things the kids had dabbled in. They believed they could walk away anytime they desired, but Satan plays for keeps and was not about to let them go easily.

He loves to get teenagers involved in the dark world because he knows they are eager and curious and if he can just get one demon into them, he thinks he has life-time followers. Paul wrote, *"Neither give place to the devil"* (*Ephesians 4:27*).

This should be a warning to us all. For we may be certain that if we give the devil a place, he will take it. If our lives are clean and we are daily walking with the Savior, we have absolutely nothing to fear. In fact, we could go so far as to say that it probably takes a lot of repeated sin and rebellion for a Christian to become controlled by a demon. The devil cannot walk in and out of our lives at will. He must first be invited in before he can take up residence in any corner of our soulish area.

Regarding the Baptism of the Spirit: I have met Christians who are terrified to ask for the baptism of the Holy Spirit for fear they will get the wrong spirit. This could not be further from the truth. We read in *Luke 11:10-13,*

> *If a son shall ask bread of any of you that is a father, will he give him a stone? Or if he ask a fish, will he for a fish give him a serpent? Or if he shall ask an egg, will he offer him a scorpion? If you then, being evil, know how to give good gifts unto your children: how much more shall your heavenly Father give the Holy Spirit to them that ask him?*

It is virtually impossible to ask for the Holy Spirit and receive an evil spirit. Likewise in our daily living, as we are looking to Jesus and trusting Him, it is not possible for an evil spirit to come into us and take possession. We are safe in God's care and we should not allow the enemy to trouble us and make us fearful in that regard.

Chapter 7

FAMILIAR SPIRITS

Look-alikes: That is exactly what a familiar spirit is, a look-alike. It assumes the appearance of another person. Especially copying those who are dead. They take on one's identity so cleverly that people are fooled into believing that the spirit they see actually is their departed loved one. Although spirit mediums have been known to sometimes use various props and methods to deceive their clients in this manner.

There have also been cases where familiar spirits have appeared. They take on the faces of those lost in death and assured the loved ones that they are in a wonderful, happy place. This deception not only gives the family assurance that their family member is all right, but it also removes their own fear of death. This, you may be sure, is a joy and delight to Satan who wants people to be unafraid in regard to their eternal destination.

In *Deuteronomy 18:10-12* we readily discover how God feels about such things as witchcraft, seances, horoscopes and such.

> *There shall not be found among you any one that makes his son or his daughter to pass through the fire, or that uses divination, or an observer of times, or an enchanter, or a witch, Or a charmer, or a consulter with familiar spirits, or a wizard, or a necromancer. For all that do these things are an abomination unto the Lord: and because of these abominations the Lord thy God does drive them out from before thee.*

Perhaps it would be well to pause long enough to take a look at some of these things.

Divination is fortune telling, consulting with images and ESP. An **observer of times** is one who uses horoscopes or astrology and an **enchanter** is one who uses omens such as tea leaves, palms, coffee grounds, jujus, and animal parts. A **witch** is someone who uses magic formulas or does incantations. A **charmer** is one who uses magic. A **consulter of mediums** is one who goes to mediums and seances for help. A **wizard** is related to the medium in practice. That is, he seeks to call up the dead. A **necromancer** is one who seeks to interrogate the dead.

All such practices are evil: In the eyes of God all the practices listed above are evil and the Christian must avoid them at all costs. Indeed, for a born-again Christian to even consider becoming involved in such things is unthinkable for they are an abomination to the Lord.

Mary, my sister, passed away, but during her last ten or fifteen years she insisted that our mother came to visit her on an ordinary basis. Mary said that our mother tweaked her toes like she did when she was alive every-time she passed her bed. She could feel her presence in her room and sometimes she would sit down and talk to her.

How could I make her believe that the devil can also tweak toes or that a demon could take on our mother's characteristics, personality and even her voice? How could I cause her to see that our mom, being a wonderful woman and a devoted Christian, would never want to run back and forth from the realms of glory to this world. I never did convince her. Mary died believing in the mystical visits from our mother.

Losing a mate: Losing a husband or wife also gives Satan excellent cause to send one of his demons to look and sound identical to that person; especially if the marriage was a happy one. A familiar spirit under the guise of the departed mate will come to comfort, to bring cheer, even guidance and advice to the one left behind. As stated before, if the marriage was exceptionally good the partner will readily accept the presence as that of the late husband or wife.

Anytime that a Christian senses that his or her mate has returned, that presence should be rebuked and resisted as something evil, otherwise they could be guilty of entertaining a demon spirit.

Co-existing with a religious spirit: A familiar spirit and a religious spirit can easily join hands and work together. For instance, a person who is zealous for God and fervently desires ministry can take to himself a religious spirit. A religious spirit will be discussed in depth in a following chapter. The religious spirit then gravitates toward ministry. The individual with a religious spirit can easily add to himself a familiar spirit as well; now there is not one, but two spirits aligned with this person.

The familiar spirit helps the religious spirit to find the ministry he longs for. It watches to see what is happening in another ministry. For example, suppose a minister is strong in prophecy; finding prophecy appealing, the familiar spirit copies it and adds it to that person's ministry. Remember familiar spirits are copiers, they copy what they see.

In the beginning, the person wanting so badly to minister was merely zealous, but in that very zeal doors have been opened to those two spirits. Now that one who so wanted ministry, wants it on a grand scale. They have prophecy so there must be more. The familiar spirit happily obliges. It sees a ministry where visions take place and so it adds visions to the religious spirit's supposed ministry. Everything the familiar spirit sees in other ministries is copied until it appears that the person who was so eager to minister has it all.

I saw just such a scenario unfold with my own eyes. A young man we shall call Mark had a ministry where the manifestations of the Spirit prevailed. To be specific, when he touched people, they fell under the power of the Spirit. A zealous older man with a mundane ministry was desperate for the power of God. So, a familiar spirit began adding manifestations. There was prophecy, and then seeing the desirable manifestations, the spirit added to the minister the ability to lay hands on people and see them fall backwards.

Mark had watched this from the beginning and was more than a little troubled by it. He cried out to God to show him what was happening and whether or not the gifts the man now exhibited were genuine. A total stranger came to his door with these words, "I am really not sure why I am here I just heard you were in the area and was impressed to come see you. As they conversed together, Mark sensed that this virtual stranger had a depth of spirit unknown by many Christians and he finally bared his soul regarding this older minister.

The newcomer nodded with understanding, "Oh, you are talking about a familiar spirit." Mark was startled and said, "But I thought familiar spirits copied dead people."

The newcomer replied, "They do, but remember, they copy what they see. It saw your ministry and began to copy it, and then added it to the other minister's life."

Light and understanding flooded Mark's mind as he realized what had happened. To the Christian who has no spiritual discernment, however, he loves the additions to the ministry that was previously so dull and applauds the man for his spiritual growth. But, were the religious and familiar spirits to suddenly depart, people would find that this particular ministry was spiritually bankrupt.

Check it out, is the anointing upon that person you believe is so wonderful? It is either the Holy Spirit or it is a pseudo anointing. That is, does it draw you to the Lord or does it draw you to the man? Do the gifts of manifestation bring you into a closer relationship with Jesus or do they make you desire more experience for experience's sake? And, that experience you received at his hands, does it make you love the Savior more or the minister more? Are all his gifts born of the Holy Spirit or do they spring from the presence of a familiar spirit? Are they used properly, and always the bottom line is do they line up with the Word of God? Does the minister exalt himself or the Lord? These are all honest and legitimate questions.

There are simply too many phonies in the world to take everything you see and hear for granted. Just because something looks good and sounds right doesn't make it so. Remember that *"...Satan himself is transformed into an angel of light. Therefore it is no great thing if his ministers also be transformed as the ministers of righteousness; whose end shall be according to their works" (2 Corinthians 11:14,15).*

A short time: Our enemy is on the prowl now as never before in the history of the world. He knows his time is short and he is constantly coming forth in new cults, new doctrines, new surprises, and the untaught Christian falls for his enticements. We simply cannot afford to be ignorant of the devil's devises. We must be alert and catch onto his tricks quickly.

Chapter 8

RELIGIOUS SPIRITS

A religious spirit is a many-faceted entity. It shows off its great depth in the Lord and must prove to everyone how spiritual it is. We see then that a religious spirit often enters the life through the sin of pride.

Look at Lucifer, Satan, director of praise, and the covering cherub, known for his exquisite beauty, his charm and wisdom. He was delegated a special place in heaven and in time he felt that he should be God. The world should fall at his feet and worship. He deserved the praise and adulation of the people of earth. "*...full of wisdom, and perfect in beauty.... You are the anointed cherub.... You have walked upon the holy mountain of God.... You were perfect in your ways.... Your heart was lifted up because of your beauty.... You have corrupted your wisdom by reason of your brightness.*" (See *Ezekiel 28:12-17.*)

God begins moving through an individual and that individual sees the awesome power and greatness of God. Indeed, he appears to have more than the ordinary Christian and pride steps in to take control.

Pride tells that person that he is chosen and highly favored of the Lord. He has anointed him with a much greater anointing than he has others. The fact that it could be a pseudo anointing never enters the mind of that one who is so taken up with his own abilities. Inwardly and outwardly that person believes that he has it all together, he can do it all and he can do it better.

A religious spirit must have the limelight to show off all his gifts and spirituality. When he is with other Christians, he clearly does all the talking, all the praying, and all the sharing. Conversation is monopolized with talk of his great spirituality.

A Christian with a religious spirit has an abundance of dreams, visions and prophecies. He dances in the spirit and doles out counsel from an endless supply of wisdom. He is used in almost all the gifts of the Spirit. In short, he can do just about anything in the spiritual realm and he always will take the glory for himself. He is preoccupied with his God-given abilities and he fails to recognize that his self-glory is an abomination to God.

An occurrence in Tucson: Years ago, I was asked to speak to a chapter of the Tucson Aglow. While at the end of the service when I was praying for people, a lady that I had never seen before walked up and began laying her hands on people with me. Since I had no idea who the woman was, I assumed incorrectly that she was a member of the Aglow Board. For that reason alone, I allowed the stranger to continue laying her hands on people for a short period of time.

The Aglow Board thought that she was with me, so they did nothing to stop her. But the Holy Spirit refuses to work where there is confusion and He simply was not moving. In fact, it seemed that He had backed away grieved.

I had already detected an alien spirit in the woman, but did not want to make waves in case she was a part of the Aglow. Since the Holy Spirit refused to work with me and since I was non-plussed as to what should be done, it was taken out of my hands. This stranger came right into my face and asked, "Do you have a word for me?" Taking a deep breath, I said, "Yes I do, please go sit down." The woman was shocked and showed it, but she obediently backed away and sat down, and immediately the Holy Spirit began to move upon those who had come for prayer. He is a Holy Spirit and simply will not move where there is strife, confusion, or the presence of some evil spirit.

Bold beyond words: A religious spirit has the boldness of a lion because it is so sure of its many capabilities. It may burst forth in tongues during the most inappropriate time of the service. This is because it disregards all rules and regulations and loves to show off. A person with such a spirit will prophesy and give words of knowledge to total strangers.

A religious spirit has a word for any person at any time of day or night. Call them on the telephone and ask them if they have a word and it will quickly tumble off their tongue. After all, he is so in tune with God that he has a word for everyone at an instant notice. People have frequently asked if I have a word for them, and nine times out of ten I do not. I tell them that God has a word for them though, and if they will just wait in His presence, He will give it to them.

There is never a need to anxiously rush about looking for a word. God still has a voice and He still knows how to speak to His people. The problem is that people do not want to take the time to listen to Him. In this day of instant everything people want instant advice also.

Example: Sasha had a history of religious spirits since she was from another country where ESP is practiced. She came to this country with a fortune-telling spirit from which she was delivered and then gave herself over to another religious spirit. This spirit was strong and loved to be seen.

At every church service after the music started, she slithered toward the front of the church, dancing and waving her arms in the air. Oldtimers were used to her, but newcomers couldn't take their eyes off of her including on prayer meeting night. For three years the pastor did nothing to correct her. The religious spirit got to show off and distract from worshipping God.

I asked her why she didn't dance in the back of the room and her reply was, "It wouldn't be the same". Big ducks in little ponds. In some instances, some people with religious spirits prefer small churches the better to show off their gifts and great spiritual qualities. Besides, it is much easier to gain a following at a little church. Seeking out hurting, oppressed people, they will gather them to themselves and teach and comfort them.

The problem is the hurting people always need ministry and the ones with religious spirits must have people to minister to. This type of situation is natural leaving most everyone satisfied.

Form of obsession: When any person begins to assume that he has some superior gift, or extraordinary power, be on the alert. This is the onset of a religious spirit's presence. Once he has the attention of an individual, and he is swayed by his charms, the spirit will subtly captivate that person. He will begin having an obsession with spiritual matters that are beyond the normal. He becomes taken up with his spirituality until he can think of little else. Eventually everything becomes something.

Example: A school nurse was oriental and became involved in false teachings and she began to change. Rather than the sweet, spiritual girl they had known before, she became nervous, flighty and super spiritual; everything was something. If the winds blew it was the Spirit moving, or if the lights blinked it was a demon in the house. Every topic of conversation was something to do with a spiritual nature. She could not talk without alluding to the spiritual. This is more than a religious spirit; it is an obsession with the spiritual.

Example: A young girl had attacked her own mother as well as attacked the pastor and his wife. God had begun to move wonderfully in the church. People were being saved and baptized in the Spirit and there was an air of excitement. This girl ran down the aisle, and grabbed the microphone from me as I was about to speak.

She said that she had a message from God. She had a religious spirit that wanted to preach and be seen and heard. I ordered her back to her seat and she refused and still yelled the same words. Eventually the usher removed her and she was later taken to jail and put in a mental institution.

In *Acts 16:17,* a girl followed Paul and Silas around proclaiming, *"These men are the servants of the most high God, which show unto us the way of salvation."* She too had a spirit of divination or fortunate telling, a first cousin of a religious spirit. It's not that they are saying things amiss, but they are always disruptive. They must have the limelight; they always have the revelation, and many times they have a mocking attitude. No matter how truly spiritual the one with them may be, the religious spirit always has the dream, the vision, the prophecy and the message.

Balance is the key: It is never pleasing to the Father for His children to go off on some tangent and become so super spiritual that they lose sight of the world they live in. Even in spiritual and doctrinal issues, we need to be balanced.

Some Christians are lopsided, and some make divine healing their entire message. While people may get healed, people don't receive salvation or get baptized in the Spirit.

68

Others are so hung up on salvation that they don't preach the deeper life. Believers are left withered and dry and yet around them others are being regenerated. Still others are so involved in deliverance their doctrine is quite literally a doctrine of demons. And, so it goes.

God wants His people to come into a place of balance. For while all matters pertaining to life and godliness are vital and important, no one issue should be lost in the shuffle. A religious spirit is always lopsided for it lives and dwells for only the spiritual, genuine or otherwise. It has little thought for the normal things of life. Eventually it becomes warped and ugly.

Should anyone reading this material suspect he has a religious spirit but doesn't quite know what to do about it, here is an excellent place to start. Try saying aloud, "I renounce this religious spirit in the name of Jesus Christ and I will not give into it again. I tell it to go in the Mighty name of Jesus, never to come against me anymore." Doubtless you must do this more than once, especially if its hold is tenacious and has been present for a time. Remember, it loves what it is doing and has no desire to leave. But as you steadfastly refuse to give it a position in your life and you continue to use authority against it, in the end it will go.

Chapter 9

WHITE WITCHCRAFT
IN THE CHURCHES

Does it exist? This sounds absurd to many. In most people's minds witchcraft cannot possibly co-exist within churches. It can and it does.

We already considered ministers who condition their people by repeating key phases and we have stated that this can indeed be done innocently in order to cause the people to retain certain knowledge. There are others, however, who do this in brain-washing the congregation. What they call out "getting it into your spirit" it can literally be a form of control. Control is always a type of witchcraft and repeating certain phrases to control and dominate is white witchcraft.

Example: Joy, a flighty young woman who was all about the presence of the Lord, "He is everywhere. God speaks to me out loud; He speaks to me from a lampshade, from a book as if it were a microphone." I warned her, but it fell on deaf ears. Satan had deceived her and she did not want to relinquish what she truly believed was the presence of God.

Talking statutes: A strange mix of truth and error in people, in almost every case, who were Christian that wanted to stay in the

Catholic Church. Error in talking statues and talking pictures goes into the occult.

Linda, a Catholic friend, told me about her and another woman, who had been praying upstairs in the church, and the presence of Jesus was sweet. She came down and passed a statue of Jesus and it changed into a statue of Mary. Then it changed back to Jesus and then back and forth. Satan was trying to deceive her and convince her that Mary and Jesus are equal, but they are not. Mary was the mother of Jesus, but Jesus alone died on the cross for our sins.

Example: A sixteen-year-old Catholic boy, Kevin, was zealous for the Lord and I spoke to him and other teens in the church, and then he took over the meeting. They turned out the lights and put lighted candles on the floor in the form of a cross. The teens sat in a circle around the candles and wove back and forth and chanted. On the wall behind them was a sign that read "the force is with us".

After the meeting, Kevin confessed to me that strange occurrences were taking place in his life when he was alone, uncanny things as though some unseen entity was trying to take possession of him. I warned Kevin about the error that he and the others were in and that they were opening themselves up to Satan, but Kevin refused to listen. He went on to tell me about a picture of Jesus that often moved and spoke to him. Sadly, he has already gone further into error.

Example: Long ago Dottie and I lived together for a while. On Christmas Eve Dottie lit up to twenty-five candles and after each one she would throw back her head and laugh. Her laughter became wild and hysterical, almost animal-like. Very bizarre and frightening.

The next day Dottie would place her hand over a hot dish and chant over it and tell it to stay hot, stay hot. At a stoplight she was telling the light to stay green using her hands in a magic wand-like action. It was demonic and witchcraft and I went to a Christian friend for advice, but he had no discernment and said that Dottie was the godliest woman he knew. This friend had no spiritual discernment.

Horoscopes and spirit guides: Surely a born-again Christian would never read or put stock in horoscopes. Some do not, unlike many pagan societies that only add Christianity to their creeds. Some Christians add horoscopes to their daily menu. Yes, they have added Christianity, but they hang on to that small corner of error that tickles their ears. They are curious to see what the future holds and are drawn to those secret and mysterious areas of the dark unknown, forbidden areas.

There are also Christians who declare they have spirit guides. In Phoenix a group of professing Christians from a well-known Evangelical church that preaches Jesus Christ, not a cult, got together to discuss spirit guides. One woman from this group said that her spirit guide revealed to her the identity of the anti-Christ and has directed her to kill him. Now the New Agers have come up with a clever plan. Knowing that most Christians would be appalled at the thought of having a spirit guide, they have appointed leaders to take groups of people into the forest to meet their angels. They lie down flat on their back and concentrate on making their spirits rise, which is astral projection, of course, and meet their angels. It sounds so spiritual, except it's not—it's occultic in the extreme.

Praying one's will on others: Though this could easily fall into the category of psychic prayer, it is also white witchcraft. All types of control in the spirit realm are forms of witchcraft. Trying to bring another individual under your control, weather it is by prayer or by persuasion, is white witchery. It's attempting to push your will on to the will of another person. This occurs in congregations, marriages, and is manifold in other relationships. Any time people are manipulated by someone into doing their will, it is witchcraft.

Visualization: The only time I have ever used visualization in any form is when I tell someone to see themselves laying something on the altar and then turning around and walking away from it. Visualization is quite big is some ministries today.

People are told to visualize the things that they desire and like, such as cars, money, houses, fame and power. But there is no place in scripture where we are to visualize anything into being. To rush headlong into visualization is to run headlong into error.

A popular TV minister ran around claiming a house for himself and in the end, he got it, but was it the will of God? *1 Timothy 6* bears careful consideration. *Hebrews 5:13, "Be content with such things as you have."*

Sarah had a strong mind, strong enough to bring others under her control. One young man discovered just how powerful she was in the realm of white witchcraft. The term "fatal attraction" is applicable in this case.

Richard met Sarah almost by accident and fell for her hard. Once under her spell, he discovered he could not get free. He had thought he could walk away when he desired, but much to his dismay, Sarah literally owned him. It seemed his very soul became irrevocably bound to her, both to her person and her every whim.

Curiously this is a combination of psychic power, a soul tie, control and witchcraft. Many times, she would command Richard to kneel before her and repeat "I love you" a hundred times.

Though he inwardly rebelled he was compelled to do as she asked. The last I heard he was unable to break the spell she had placed upon him.

Witchcraft takes many forms. But that it does exist in some charismatic and other Christian circles is a fact and only those with the gift of discerning of spirits can sift through the rubbish and ferret it out. May God give us those dedicated Christians who are to be scorned and misunderstood as they probe into the shifting sands of error and uncover that which is deceiving to people.

Chapter 10

THE LAYING
ON OF HANDS

An age-old ritual, the ministry of the laying on of hands is nearly as old as time. In *Leviticus 16:21*, Aaron was instructed to lay both his hands upon the head of a live goat and confess over it the sins of the people. In *Mark 16:18,* Jesus said you should lay hands on the sick and they will recover. Over and over Jesus laid his hands upon people and they were healed instantly.

In *1 Timothy 5:22*, we read, *"Lay hands suddenly on no man, neither be partaker of other men's sins: keep thyself pure."* Particular note should be taken of that last part, for it would appear that in our day many ignore, or have forgotten, that admonition.

God had a special reason for telling us not to suddenly lay hands on an individual. To begin with, unless we are under the anointing of the Holy Spirit, whatever spirit is at work in the other person's life can turn and attack the one praying. It can't enter, but it can attack.

For instance, disregarding the fact that you are not under the anointing, you decide to move in presumption and lay hands on someone anyway. Say the person upon whom you lay your hands is battling the spirit of lust. Since you are not under the anointing, unreasonable and mysterious lust takes hold of you. You have become open prey to that spirit. It sees that your defenses are down and so it immediately tries to attach itself to you. You, not understanding what has occurred, begin to literally cave in under that spirit.

What happened is simple; you laid your hands upon an individual with the spirit of lust. You were not under the anointing which is your protection and you became a partaker of their sin.

The scripture is given to us in three distinct parts. *"Lay hands suddenly on no man; be not a partaker of other men's sins, and keep thy self-pure."* Now sinful thoughts fill your mind and the temptation is strong to yield to them. The battle begins.

You must round up these thoughts like ragged prisoners of war and bring them into subjection. This is a costly lesson, but it is one you will remember long after the victory has been won. By the same token, great harm can be accomplished when you receive the laying on of hands by someone who is not under the anointing. I have left the altar of prayer to avoid the wrong laying on of hands.

We impart what is in us. *Acts 8:17* says, *"Then laid they their hands on them, and they received the Holy Ghost."* The reason they received the Holy Spirit is because that is what the apostles had to impart. Never forget that you impart what you have. If someone wants to lay hands on you, be certain that what they have to offer is what you want to receive. One can only impart or transmit what is in them. When Peter and John went to the temple to pray, they encountered a lame man who pled for money. But Peter said, *"such as I have give I thee" (Acts 3:6)*.

A spirit in Dixie, a friend of my prayer partner, wanted to lay hands on me and pray for me. But I saw something in Dixie's eyes that troubled me and I was concerned and trapped in an awkward situation and I acquiesced. Something happened as a result of Dixie's prayer that I was to fight that nearly cost me my ministry.

I had always been able to speak with ease from the pulpit, but now it was a different story. I felt sheer terror. A man-fearing spirit bound me and I wanted to flee for my life. After getting back home and in the presence of Dixie again, I looked into her eyes and I realized Dixie had a man-fearing spirit. I asked Dixie if she was afraid to speak before people, "Yes," she said. "I break down completely just giving a simple testimony: I am simply scared to death." Now I understood what I had been fighting through Dixie by her merely laying hands on me. A man-fearing spirit had attached itself to me and its intent was to destroy me and my ministry if possible. It was time for war.

I bound the spirit of fear and loosed myself from its clutches. I tore down the stronghold Satan had built against me in Jesus' powerful name. I adamantly refused the spirit of fear and claimed *2 Timothy 1:7, "For God has not given us the spirit of fear; but of power, and of love, and of a sound mind."*

Release did not come instantly, but the next time I entered a pulpit, I was free. God has provided us with implements of warfare, but it is up to us to use them. The instruments listed in the *6th chapter* of *Ephesians* are highly effective in this war against the enemy of our souls. It is impossible to gain victory by means of ordinary methods. For our adversary is invisible and must be dealt with by supernatural means. *"For the weapons of our warfare are not carnal, but mighty through God to the pulling down of strong holds" (2 Corinthians 10:4).* Add to these then the name of Jesus, the blood He shed on Calvary, and the Word of God and we have an arsenal that causes Satan to flee.

Promiscuous laying on of hands: This is the most dangerous practice and is as dangerous as ministering without the anointing.

Yet we see it constantly. People are constantly told to lay hands on the person next to you. But nine-nine out of every one-hundred of those who consent to that are not under the anointing and know little about it.

At best, their hands are empty and can impart nothing from God. And at worst they can transmit to the next person whatever spirit is in them. This attitude is many times taken with ministers; the concept is, you have prayed for everyone else; now let us pray for you." That is fine if you know everyone's spirit, but if you are in a place where the people are unknown to you, it is far better to decline the offer. Sad to say, but in my previous church I saw total strangers walk in off the street and participate in the laying on of hands in prayer lines. Unknown, and usually uninvited, they would step forward when a prayer line was being conducted and take part. As Paul would say, *"Brethren these things ought not to be so".*

The late William Branham, who at the end of his life was in deep error, had laid hands on Mary and soon thereafter she began knowing things supernaturally. She attended my church and the pastor asked me to pay her a visit, which I did, and I learned a great deal.

Mary told me that the mailman was coming while still down the street and she stated that he was going to leave her a brochure about the Holy Land, which he did. It was a windy day in March, but to Mary the wind was the Spirit. Mary told me that the Lord wanted her to go to the Holy Land and be baptized in the Jordan River and I was to go along as her spokeswoman.

We would stand on Mt. Moriah before an altar and black snakes would be crawling around. This went on and on and it became increasingly frightening. Mary wanted to pray with me before I left. She told me things about my son that she could not have possibly have known—his age and hair and eye color, and where he was at that time.

Many assume that just because an individual can "read your mail" as it were, that it has to be God; no, it doesn't. It does not necessarily have to be the word of knowledge just because a person knows things about you.

Same in fortune telling and other forms of divination which will always interject an element of truth in order to deceive. I will never forget the violent wind that day that beat upon Mary's house as though legions of evil spirits had been loosed upon her home. I learned later that it had been William Branham, known at that time for having a spirit of divination, who had laid hands on her and that same spirit had been imparted. Again, the spirit that is in you is the spirit you are going to impart.

Healing: My daughter Lynn, at age eight, was diagnosed by nine doctors as having cancer of the brain. It was in the cerebellum where it could not be removed, but they were going to operate, get a smear and see if it would respond to cobalt treatment.

She was duly given six-and-a-half months to live. I asked a spirit-filled minister to go to the hospital and pray for Lynn before surgery. He did, along with some men from his church. They anointed her with oil and laid hands on her for healing. The doctors shaved Lynn's head and drilled holes in her skull and she was in surgery for eight hours. The cancer had vanished. She was never touched again.

Example: I laid hands on a man who was oozing from eczema. After the service, he took his family to Macdonald's and using his hands to express himself was shocked to see that he was completely healed. Something about touch; indeed, there is just something about the power of touch. When hands are anointed of the spirit, wonderful things take place, blessings follow, sickness flees, oppression lifts, people receive the baptism. The world is crying out for a compassionate touch.

I have witnessed strong men break down and weep like babies under the power of touch. Wounds in the spirit are frequently healed because of someone's compassionate hand. In the Bible spiritual gifts were imparted in this manner. It says in *1 Timothy 4:14, "Neglect not the gift that is in thee, which was given thee by prophecy, with the laying on of the hands of the presbytery".*

The first time I knew anything about the laying on of hands was when the Southern Baptist church we attended called us forward and the minister and other men laid their hands on us and sent us away to Bible School. In meetings, I would single out those who I felt had the greatest potential for yielding to God for His anointing.

Then, after I had prayed for someone and then moved on, one of the people would take over to keep the anointing on them until God had accomplished His work in their lives. Remember, it is the anointing that breaks the yoke. See *Isaiah 10:27. "And it shall come to pass in that day, that his burden shall be taken away from off thy shoulder, and his yoke from off they neck, and the yoke shall be destroyed because of the anointing."*

Lepers: I have always been awed by the story of Jesus touching the leper for this was one who was not touched. A leper was a social outcast forced to live in loneliness and isolation. When he approached a town, he was compelled to cry the words "unclean, unclean" so people could scramble from his path. Yet Jesus touched such a man. Could it be because He knew the man's desire for human touch? After all, Jesus could have but spoken a word. There was no need to touch him, but He did touch him and through His touch the leper was made whole, body soul and spirit.

But Lord, a rooster? It was one of the first healings that I had ever seen. I was staying in a pastor's home and a dog had attacked the rooster and left him a bloody mess. The pastor brought the rooster into the kitchen. I dreamed that the rooster was well and the next morning I got up and laid hands on the rooster and in the middle of the night he flapped his wings and crowed. He was completely healed and returned to the hen house.

At another time, I was shot in a freak accident and a bullet passed through my body twice. The first night in the hospital, heavily sedated, the Holy Spirit alerted me that there was a stranger by my bed. In the natural, nothing short of an earthquake could have aroused me.

The Holy Spirit alerted me that a demonic spirit was near; the man was someone I had never met before and I knew there would be some sort of altercation. "I have come to lay hands on you for healing," he said. I said, "No, I have already had the laying on of hands." He said, "I am going to lay hands on you again." I replied, "No you are not!" and I pushed the button for the nurse. With that, the man turned and like an apparition of the night vanished from sight. His parting words were, "I'll get you yet." Four days later I went into the church where I had been scheduled to speak and there was the man who had entered my hospital room. The facts were that the man lived in a broken-down station wagon with a girl and sold drugs. The man was full of evil spirits. Oh! The faithfulness of the Holy Spirit that memorable night! That He had awakened me from a heavily drugged sleep, which was amazing, in order to alert me of danger and to protect me, was mind boggling

When we are unable to avoid it, when we are caught in situations where we cannot avoid the wrong laying on of hands, we should always plead the blood of Jesus Christ for protection, and even when we don't feel like it.

My husband and I had been called to pray for people who wanted the baptism in the Holy Spirit. I had felt quite spiritual and then abruptly I felt cold and unworthy and wanted to stay home. God had been using us and I didn't want to visit these people. I went into the family room to turn off the light, and the stereo was on and I accidentally touched it with my fingers. Surprisingly, it grew very loud and clear, and when I removed my hand, it was muted.

My hand had acted like an antenna supplying energy to the unit. I said to the Lord, "I feel cold in my spirit tonight, but I give you my hands to use for your glory. I felt nothing when I touched the stereo but the effect was obvious. So, I concluded that my feelings did not count as we went to visit the people. I asked God to allow me to be His antenna as we went forth.

As a result, the night of that simple illustration, God did use my hands. One lady received the in-filling of the Holy Spirit and another was released from the bondage of oppression. The anointing is a protective shield and it is always prudent to ask for anointing before laying hands on someone. If, on the other hand, you are cornered into receiving the laying on of hands from someone unknown to you, then the blood of Jesus becomes your shield. If you are in your home church where you are sure of everyone, you can give yourself willingly to this sacred rite.

Chapter 11

FOUR STRIKING LEVELS

Satan is aware that boundaries have been placed before him. He can come just so close and no closer. However, his desire is to keep the believer ignorant of these boundaries so he lashes out again and again. Some of his attacks are bluff, but more often than not they are deadly serious. He wants us to believe that he has the power to override our wills and destroy us. But remember, he can come only as close as we allow him to come.

There are four levels that Satan aims his arrows of attack and the first of these is depression. For most, depression relates to happenings. If bad things happen, or if plans fail to emerge as we hoped, we are plunged into the blackness of depression. We are consumed by a heavy sickness and sink into the "sigh of despondency." This sensation is described with feelings such as sadness, cast down, darkness, and rejection; to feel low and dull in spirit.

Satan delights in bringing such fears upon the Christian for he knows a discouraged, hopeless Christian is no threat to his kingdom. He makes them feel isolated and they believe no one else has ever felt the way they are now feeling. There is no light at the end of the tunnel and nothing they feel is ever going to change.

Depression is a deadly foe and must be overcome. When David was depressed, the Bible states that he was greatly depressed. In *1 Samuel 30:6, "And David was greatly distressed;*

for the people spoke of stoning him, because the soul of all the people was grieved, every man for his sons, and for his daughters: but David encouraged himself in the Lord his God."

He recounted the many times God had proven Himself faithful. The times He had provided for David, the times He had saved his life and perhaps the sins God had forgiven. Just so, when the enemy attempts to bring depression upon us, we need to encourage ourselves in the Lord. He has never failed us; He has never failed to bring us through in victory. Therefore, He will not fail us now.

Bonnie: She was one of the saddest cases I had ever encountered, and although she appeared to love the Lord, she was manic-depressive. To escape the dark mood swings, she had more than once tried to take her life. Once she brought a live radio into her bathtub hoping to get electrocuted. The sad part is, to elevate herself from the depression she had begun drinking. She no longer attended church because it was too much to cope with.

If we would allow him that space, Satan would do that to every one of us. He would dull our thoughts and depress our spirits and cause us to be lethargic and uncaring. But when depression strikes, and it strikes nearly everyone at one time or another, then it is imperative that we take up the Word of God and strike back. *"There has no temptation taken you but such as is common to man: but God is faithful, who will not suffer you to be tempted above that you are able; but will with the temptation also make a way to escape, that you may be able to bear it"* (1 Corinthians 10:13). Take up the sword of the spirit which is the word of God and begin doing battle against the depression the enemy has brought into your life.

Oppression: This is the second striking level and it is deeper than depression. It is the presence of an evil spirit leaning its presence against you. And, it can at times be deep enough to show in the eyes of an individual.

Oppression comes against the mind and spirit to such a degree that the one afflicted can lose the desire to smell a rose or watch the magic of a sunset. The natural normal things of life become meaningless and the person may find themselves simply sitting and staring into space; for if depression is darkness, oppression is black and brooding.

My daughter came under heavy oppression after a visit from a Hindu neighbor. Like trailing wisps of black fog, it pressed against her until she could hardly speak. I drove to her house and prepared to do battle. As soon as I entered the home, a tight band formed around her house and the heaviness in the air was charged—almost electric—with some magical presence. It was difficult to think, or even breathe, and we both had to fight to stave off the mental confusion that would have consumed us.

We went through the home armed with olive oil, anointing every door and every window, and even the sofa where the neighbor had sat. By the authority of the Word of God and the blood of Jesus we commanded evil to flee. Within twenty minutes the air was clear and the house was free. The oppression had completed lifted.

The problem is that so many either fail to understand the power of such an alien spirit or they become so consumed by the oppression, they forget to fight against it. I have met Christians that have lived under oppression for so long they can hardly function.

Kate cared for me when I was sick with TB. She had previously had a spiritual breakdown. Kate had been so harassed and oppressed by Satan that her nerves had broken, not knowing how to combat the enemy.

Oppression must be withstood. It saps the strength and steals the joy from one's life. It transforms happy, out-going Christians into shriveled lifeless robots that go through the daily grind in dull automation. This is a deadly foe and must be overcome and authority taken over it immediately.

The longer it clings to the individual the more difficult it is to gain victory over it. Sometimes one must confide in a trusted friend and, as you take authority together, it is easier to come out from under the insidious darkness of oppressive forces. Remember, *"That if two of you shall agree on earth as touching any thing that they shall ask, it shall be done for them of my Father which is in heaven"* (Matthew 18:19).

Obsession: This is the third and deeper level of attack. Obsession is fixation. It is being utterly taken up by one thing. For instance, on a talk show a lady was obsessed with a ball team. This fixation, or obsession, was so extreme that her home was done in the colors of the team. She wore the team's uniform and kept her husband in a constant state of humiliation. And when they attended a game together, she dawned a little nose mask to root for the team. A vast array of mementos adorned their home, all relics of past games. Some of it had been brought to the talk show, helmets, mugs, pictures, shirts, and cups.

Obsession takes on different forms. Sometimes an individual is consumed by one topic of a conversation. You try to steer them into other channels and they will manage to bring the conversation right back to the one thing that they are obsessed with. Sorne people are obsessed with hobbies, such as bordering strongly on being obsessed with rebuilding guns, fishing, or ham

86

radios. They seemly to do little else. Anything that steals our attention to the exclusion of everything else is obsession.

Leann was obsessed with the demonic world. The demonic realm was all that interested her, all she wanted to talk about and all she read about. The result was she became a mentally oppressed Christian.

There are entire groups of Christians that sit around and only talk about Satan and his works. It is dangerous, unhealthy, and Satan loves it. He is getting the glory that he feels he so richly deserves. Such people are more taken up with Satan than with God.

Any time one becomes too interested in demons and spends too much time exploring the realm of darkness, they are opening themselves up to the possibility of a demonic presence fastening itself upon their life. I have seen believers so mentally oppressed that you would think they had been in Caanan Land eating sour grapes. They are themselves miserable and cannot be a good witness to an unbeliever.

Who needs it? The unbeliever has enough problems already. There are two major reasons for this. When oppression struck, instead of fighting they bowed down to it and allowed it to take control over them. The other reason is some Christians actually take delight in speaking of Satan and the work of demons.

Two much curiosity regarding the spirit realm is never healthy. God told us what we need to know and to explore; beyond that is simply not good. Remember the one you talk about most is the presence you invite into your life.

Doctrine: Multitudes of ministers come under obsession unwittingly. Sorne ministers only talk about healing, people are healed but rarely born again. Others speak only about salvation so people are saved, but no one is filled with the Holy Spirit. Still others only have one agenda—getting people filled with the Holy Spirit. So, while many are supposedly "baptized in the Spirit" no one is saved or healed.

So many preachers today are hung up on riches and to delve into this in depth would require a book. Suffice it to say, however, that is the singular message. "God wants you to be rich." This is their cry and it smacks of such rank error that frankly, it stinks. Yet multitudes are drawn into its alluring promises of wealth.

Again, balance in all things is the key to a happy existence. Christ must be the focal point and all else must revolve around Him, *Malachi 3:16* states, *"Then they that feared the Lord spake often one to another: and the Lord hearkened, and heard it."*

Allowing the dark ways of depression, oppression and/or obsession to consume us is not necessary. That would be to say that God left us defenseless and open prey to the enemy of our souls. We must strike back with the weapons that He has given us. He has assured our victory if only we fight back and never forget *Luke 10:19* says *"Behold, I give unto you power to tread on serpents and scorpions, and over all the power of the enemy: and nothing shall by any means hurt you."*

Possession: This is Satan's ultimate goal, for evil spirits require one thing in order to accomplish their work effectively and that is a body to dwell in and function through. If Satan cannot have you for himself, the next best thing is for his emissaries to take up residence in your life.

Then he can not only make your life miserable, but can, to a large degree, control your actions. We must refer once again to *Ephesians 4:27,* which states simply, *"neither give place to the devil."*

If it were not possible for Christians to give him place, Paul would never have admonished us not to. The individuals in the following scenarios are not Christians, but believers can open themselves up to demon possession we have discussed. Let me reiterate, however, the spirit cannot be possessed: it is bought with the blood of Jesus, for when the door is open in some soulish area, it is an invitation for an evil spirit to come and take control.

It may not happen the first time the door is open or even the second time, but as the door is left available an evil spirit will sooner or later take advantage of it. A spirit in the soulish area will, of course, soon manifest itself in the physical body. We have only to look at some of the fallen creatures to understand these things can happen to Christians.

As an example, let us suppose that a minister is obsessed with porn magazines and movies. A door has been left ajar for a spirit of lust to enter. Eventually that person's thoughts will come under the dominion of that spirit, and at another time that spirit will manifest itself in the physical. It may be masturbation, adultery, perversion or even rape, but in some way that spirit will make its presence in the life known; for it must be satisfied.

If a person lies to free himself from an undesirable situation, again not necessarily a believer, a door has been opened. If his lies continue over a period of time, a lying spirit can take up residence. In time that person may not be able to tell the truth.

A young girl who had a lying spirit and who, even if her mother had evidence in her hands to the contrary, the girl would lie with tears pouring down her face. She was a Christian and some years later, as she was walking along on a sidewalk, told God that she wanted to be free of it and started retching, and has been free of that spirit ever since.

Some people become pathological liars and they can spin yarns faster than the human brain can think them up. Some people give in to drink. If the drinking habit continues over a period of time, an alcoholic demon will enter that individual making life miserable for the entire family. His eyes will become unnaturally bright and glaring and his family will begin to see another entity in the eyes of the man who was once so loving.

An aura of protection: Is it true or even possible that we have an aura of protection? George C. Ritchie in his book "Return from Tomorrow" believes we do. Dr. Ritchie is a psychiatrist who died at eighteen in an army hospital.

Early in life he had received Christ as his Savior and relates that when he died the Lord appeared to him and took him on an amazing journey. They made many stops, at least one of which was later identified when he visited the area as a well man. A major stop was in a bar where men were drinking heavily.

He tells of a luminescence glow that surrounded the men and says that the glow moved when they moved like a second skin. All around the drinking men were disembodied beings, spirits that did not possess the second skins.

Though the men were unaware of the disembodied ones among them, the spirits appeared to be desperately thirsty and franticly attempted to gain possession of their glasses of whiskey. He naturally decided that the cocoon of life was the property of living people only.

He saw a sailor rise falteringly to his feet and take a few steps only to fall heavily to the floor. After this occurred, the cocoon of light around him opened at the very top of his head and slid away from his head and shoulders. At that moment one of the disembodied beings hovering nearby leaped on top of the sailor.

In lightning-quick motion the beings that had been watching the sailor drink and who appeared to have a great thirst for his whiskey sprang and instantly disappeared inside the young man on the floor. Whereas before the disembodied ones had needlessly groped for the whiskey glasses in the hands of these men, the moment the men were out of control and too drunk to function, instead of there being two figures there was only one.

The beings that had no second skin simply dove inside the drunken men and vanished. Dr. Richie saw this happen over and over. A man would collapse in drunkenness and the aura would open up and one of the beings would instantly spring inside. Now is it possible that this is how people become possessed? They give themselves over to something so often and so thoroughly that they are out of control and that is when the spirit dives inside.

I cannot from experience tell you how it all works. Perhaps we are protected by some aura and when we give ourselves repeatedly to sin, an opening is made for some spirit to enter. I leave this for your consideration.

Things to do: No matter in which level you are, you can listen to anointed music. The advantages are innumerable. You can claim the Word of God, and stand behind what He has written. You can plead the blood. You can make deliberate choices on things that can change your situation. God will always be present to strengthen your resolve. You can be free no matter how active the enemy may be in your life. There is no well of darkness so black that the Son of God cannot lift you out as you call upon His Name. Remember the weapons of our warfare.

Remember Vickie who fasted and prayed for her own deliverance and swiftly the Lord moved on her behalf? Never forget that there is not a demon from hell that can hold you for long when you truly want to be free.

SUPPLEMENTATION

Betty Swinford was instrumental in imparting much of this information to my co-laborer, Jeannette Haley. When the Lord put us together in ministry, Jeannette imparted it to me.

I had the great privilege of meeting Betty and watching her minister. She was a powerhouse. God moved, demons manifested, and people were healed and set free. The times I spent with her allowed me the blessed opportunity of being able to also call her "my friend."

Before I met her, I was warned that when she looked at you, you felt she was seeing in every area of your life, leaving you feeling undone, vulnerable, and exposed. Possessing a sense of humor, she laughed at such a notion that she was privy to such matters and assured me that unless the Holy Spirit revealed something to her, she saw nothing and knew nothing.

I remember even confessing to her a particular time I had been in rebellion. She showed such grace as she quietly listened to my confession while I repented before the Lord making peace with Him.

However, I had to note her eyes did not appear to see much of this world. You could tell that she had seen into another world. She had experienced its power, encountered its incredible authority, and at times walked in its glory. She reminded me of a person whose desire was to be faithful to the end, while tightly holding on to the time when she would bathe in her Lord's unhindered glory and experience unending, wondrous fellowship with Him.

The thing that surprised me the most about Betty was her theme. Every minister has their particular emphasis when it comes to their message. For Betty, it was not ministry, power, deliverance, and the Holy Spirit (even though she knew Him well), but that one could truly know God for themselves.

Jeannette and I have both been in ministry together since 1989. It is obvious that through the years we have greatly benefitted from Betty's insight on this subject, but we also had some experiences that we felt might bring some additional insight to the reader on each subject addressed in this book. This is our way to not only show how Betty's work has followed her, but it has multiplied and produced precious fruit as well.

To identify our different experiences our initials, RK for myself and JH for Jeannette are used after each story.

Chapter 1: Discerning of Spirits

1) We are to test the spirit behind all things (*1 John 4:1*). We must understand what constitutes spirit. Spirit is determined by motive, which entails agendas and priorities (*Proverbs 16:2*), intention (*Hebrews 4:12*), which for the believer is to bring glory to God and not to themselves or others, and the right goal or target which should be to always lift up Jesus so men can flee the wrath of God and be saved (*John 12:32*). The main way to test the spirit is to discern the quality of fruit, which determines the environment that it creates (*Matthew 7:16, 20*).

Example: Many years ago, Rayola and I lived in an old farmhouse in Idaho. It was the only place we could barely afford to live. The upstairs gave me a great "north light" area in which to paint, and the other room was Rayola's bedroom. When we moved in, I sensed a "presence" in that room, which we prayed against. Later, we met a lady, who, when she discovered where we lived, asked if we had "met" the spirit that lived in the upstairs bedroom, and when she learned we had, she said, "Well, don't get rid of it because it's friendly." There is no such thing as a "friendly" spirit or demon, and yes, we commanded it to leave and it did. (JH)

2) Paul tells us in *1 Corinthians 2:11-14* that there are three main spirits in this world: *Holy Spirit, natural spirit (the old man), and the spirit of the world (Satan).*
3) The Holy Spirit is the only right spirit, while the other two are both wrong spirits, but to address the two wrong spirits properly we must even discern between them. In the case of Peter in *Matthew 16:22-23* and Judas Iscariot in *John 13:26-27*, the spirit was identified as being that of Satan but when it came to John and James in *Luke 9:52-56*, it was their natural spirit in operation. We are told in *Proverbs 25:28, "He that hath no rule over his own spirit is like a city that is broken down, and without walls."* There is no resistance against the spirit of the world, Satan, if our own spirit is not under the discipline and leading of the Holy Spirit.

Example: I was ministering to a woman who was struggling with personal issues. However, it seemed as if I was hitting an invisible wall. It was clear nothing was penetrating into her understanding and I felt the life being sucked out of me. In seeking the Lord, He showed me that the wall was demonic. It was then I realized that if you are dealing with a person in rebellion, they will emotionally fluctuate, but if it is demonic, you will hit an immovable wall and you must take authority over it so that you can once again reach that person to be ministered to. (Note: There is no reasoning with a demon.) (RK)

4) The natural spirit is what we toy with in our mind when it comes to our lusts and desires. We give it audience as it entices us with the possibilities of how something will make us feel, and once we give into the temptation, it leads to sin and some type of ruin (*James 1:12-16*).

5) Satan's attacks come from without and are like terrible darts of poison (wiles-tricks of Satan) that suddenly hit or intrude into our mind *(Ephesians 6:11, 16)*. They immediately cause confusion in us as to how we could think such things, and ends in condemnation because we have been defiled by them. However, they are lies, and for them to have a devastating impact on us, we must come into agreement with them by believing they are our thoughts when in fact they are darts from Satan.

Example: I was pretty much minding my own business and trying to finish a project one day when these terrible immoral images and thoughts came into my mind. I was shocked at the intrusion and was confused as to how they could even be present. After all, it was not in my heart to give such things any type of audience. I realized they were not mine and I needed to rebuke them and send them back to their source. As soon as I took authority over them, my mind cleared, confusion dissipated and my soul and spirit were at ease once again. We must always remember our God is not a God of confusion and when Satan insert his lies or wickedness in something it will immediately cause confusion to the saint (*1 Corinthians 14:33*). (RK)

6) We must *repent* of giving way to the temptations of the natural spirit while taking *authority* over the darts of Satan *(Luke 13:3, 5; Luke 10:17-20)*. The problem is people try to repent of Satan's darts while trying to take authority over the flesh. This will prove to be ineffective. We are to overcome the flesh through repentance of our ways, brokenness over sin, and humility before God. In Christ, we are more than victors or conquerors over Satan, but we must stand in the Lord's power as we submit to His authority while lifting up the sword of the Word of God to resist all of Satan's attempts to cause us to bow to his lies, ways, and doings *(James 4:5-10)*.

Example: There was one woman we worked with that was greatly oppressed. She faithfully went to church and even had books on spiritual deliverance, but she was miserable and tormented. Even though I knew others had prayed for her deliverance, we agreed to pray with her. As we stood in the gap, we witnessed that at times she would close down and other times she responded as if she was greatly insulted. The Lord showed me that when she was closed down, the demons were active and when she was insulted it was because her natural spirit was taking offence for the rebuke that was taking place against the work of darkness in her life. We later learned she was in an adulterous affair with a married man and she did not want to repent; therefore, Satan had both an inroad and right to enslave her and make her existence miserable. (RK)

Chapter 2: Declaration of War

1) A missionary from Africa shared how an African man came to her and thanked her for sending missionaries to their country

but was puzzled due to the ignorance of Christians in America and their denial concerning the demonic world and their unwillingness and ineptness to admit it exists and address it. The Bible is clear, we live in Satan's world, and he has his ranks of minions, whether principalities over nations, powers over governments, or rulers of darkness over the world's systems. Wickedness clearly reigns in all high places where righteousness is not the gauge (*2 Corinthians 4:3-4; Ephesians 6:12*).

Example: After conducting a retreat, we invited women to step forward to be prayed for. One woman had already approached me and confessed that she was hindered from moving forward in her Christian walk. I looked into her eyes and did not discern any demonic oppression and suggested she come up for prayer after the meeting.

When she came forward, I gave a summary of what she had told me to Jeannette. Immediately, Jeannette pointed a finger at her and declared she had a hindering spirit. Upon exposing the source of oppression, the demonic entity lifted the lady up and slammed her flat onto the floor. For the next two hours we dealt with the manifestations of the demonic world from tremendous strength that kept her glue to the floor until it was rebuked in the mighty name of Jesus. We watched the demon try to strangle her, as a sulfur smell abounded, and her brown eyes changed to a swampy green. Her body parts contorted in unnatural ways. When the demonic oppression lifted, she admitted that she thought demons were like leprechauns. Ignorance towards the demonic realm may keep us in blissful denial, but it is a darkness that allows Satan and his realm to go unchecked, unchallenged,

98

and will remain successful in keeping a Christian from going forward in their spiritual life. The Bible is clear about demonic activity; therefore, ignorance about such matters is a matter of choice and assumption. Keep in mind, to be ignorant of Satan's device is a form of disobedience because Paul exhorted us in 2 *Corinthians 2:11, "Lest Satan should get an advantage of us: for we are not ignorant of his devices."* (RK)

2) Americans think they are too cultured to be plagued by the demonic world like those of pagan cultures. This is one of Satan's great deceptions (*John 8:44*). In our way of thinking, our ways are refined and not pagan; therefore, we can't imagine that they are all that bad or wrong. Reformation of the outward is not transformation and revival of the inward.

Culture may cultivate in such a way we may maintain certain outward protocols and conducts that make us appear refined, but paganism is not just a matter of practices, but of attitudes that will condone that which is idolatrous and wicked. At such times we may cover up our spiritual pigpens with an appearance of righteousness; thereby, covering up demonic activities, but it will never do away with them. Only the blood of Jesus will draw the line between Satan's encroachment in our lives as believers, and cleanse us from all unrighteousness, while closing all avenues, entrances, and doors to him. Paul was an overcomer because he chose to die daily to self, while keeping his body in subjection to the Spirit and becoming crucified to the world and the world to him (*Romans 12:1-2; 1 Corinthians 9:24-27; 15:31; Ephesians 2:13-18; Galatians 6:14; 2 Timothy 3:5; 1 John 1:7-9*).

Our civilized ways may make wickedness look cultured, but in God's sight it is still wicked. However, those pagan cultures understand how the unseen world works, and in their need to understand the unexplainable they have tapped into the demonic realm and know how powerful it is. Once they become Christians, they understand the church is in a war. It is not between countries, political parties, races, religions, etc., rather it is between two kingdoms: good and evil, darkness and light, and the dividing line of the cross of Christ stands between two results: curses or blessings, and life or death *(Deuteronomy 30:19-20).*

Example: I had a hard time believing what I was hearing. The woman on the other end of the phone, after confessing she had been in covens for years, was looking forward to hell because Satan promised his followers that a room in hell had been prepared for them where they would be able to rest.

The reality for those who serve Satan is nothing but the soul being constantly driven by obsessive lusts, restlessness of the spirit, wicked imaginations that have no limit to exploring the depths of evil, torment of the mind, and non-ending gross and indescribable rituals that produced thick spiritual darkness. I immediately took her to the Word of God and showed her that the torment she was experiencing in her life would follow her even in greater measure into hell and that what she desired was heaven. She admitted she didn't want to go to hell, rather she wanted to go to heaven.

She did travel by plane for ministry. We learned that God reached down through the darkness and told her to leave the coven, and being a compliant servant that never questioned an order, she did so but not without great cost. It cost her the only son that had survived the sacrifice of three of her other children to Satan. The coven murdered him because she had left it, but God later stopped their plans to murder her.

That was not all she had to wade through. She went to churches who recognized her from a popular national TV talk show where she, along with the leader of the church of Satan, Anton LaVey lied about sacrificing children. The leaderships of the different churches told her to come late and leave early, but none of them wanted to answer her questions or stand in the gap.

Twelve years after her journey began, she sat in our living room and you know what set her free? It started when she believed the Word of God about heaven. She had to step over paralyzing fear as she risked being rejected, judged, and criticized when she came to us to change her direction, but real freedom was realized because she chose to believe the Word of God. The One she was told to hate she turned to with her heart, out of faith towards His promises, and asked Him save her, deliver her, heal her, and set her free from the entanglements of Satan. And in the end, she was not ashamed in believing God would, for He is NOT A LIAR and was faithful to His Word and saved her. (RK)

3) Satan has declared war on God and His people. The problem is, many Christians in America have not engaged in the war that rages outside of their small religious worlds to face their enemies; therefore, the enemies have come into homes, churches, schools, and societies without much, if any, opposition at all. Sadly, we have been conditioned by Satan's systems to just roll with the wicked tides coming into our society because, after all, what can we do about it?

EXAMPLE: Years ago, when visiting a certain church in Montana, the pastor and his wife invited the church to come to what was, if

I remember correctly, a type of house-warming. As I walked down the hallway to the bathroom, I suddenly sensed a presence. It was quite strong, so I took the wife aside and asked her if she had ever sensed a demon in their hallway. Her eyes grew wide, and she said, "Yes, but we don't know what to do about it." I was taken aback that they had no clue of their authority in Christ! Thankfully, they were willing to gather the people and have it cast out of their home. (JH)

4) We have been called to be soldiers but how many have been trained to stand, withstand, and to continue to stand in order to endure the attacks upon our faith, our testimony, our home and other sacred institutions *(Ephesians 6:10-14; 2 Timothy 2:3-4; Jude 3; Revelation 12:11)*? It is important to point out we have not been called to take new territory but to ensure the integrity and quality of the territory that we claim already belongs to God: our souls, lives, homes, and churches.

Example: Demons are real, and they do bizarre things. One time when my husband and I were in his pickup, sitting at a red light, each thinking our own thoughts, I felt a tap on the top of my head. I turned to ask him why he tapped me on the top of the head, and took note that his hands had not moved from their position on the steering wheel. Before I could open my mouth to ask him about it, he blurted out, "How come you tapped me on the top of my head?" He was clearly annoyed. I said, "I was just going to ask you the same thing!" I would have had to scoot closer to him to even reach the top of his head, and he would've seen me. It was just one of those bizarre things that you remember, but can't really explain. Another incident involved the strange appearance of three red scratches resembling claw marks that suddenly appeared on a friend's back where she could not have possible reached herself, neither could she recall feeling them the day before. Then the middle of her body broke out into a serious occurrence of shingles that lasted for almost a year. Can demons touch you? Apparently so. A man Rayola and I visited, who had grown up in a coven and was dedicated to a strong spirit guide, had genuinely received Christ and come out of witchcraft, but a demon still had the power to pick him up and throw him across his room and up against the wall. This was a very tall, strong man. He sought deliverance from it for years before he finally received it in a certain church by the mercy of God. (JH)

5) We have been given armor in *Ephesians 6:11-17* but how many know how to put it on properly. After all, our "undergarments" must be humility according to *1 Peter 5:5*, and our belt of truth must be firmly in place for the rest of the armor to properly fit. We have a sword, but how much is it used as "friendly fire" against those who are allies, often buffeting and wounding God's servants in their execution of their duties?

EXAMPLE: When I heard this story, I couldn't help but relate it to the spiritual realm. A woman told me that one day as she was sitting on the porch, she heard quite a commotion occurring so she turned to see her small dog yelping and running as fast as he could while behind the dog followed turkeys who were also running while making their distress known, and behind them was her little grandson with a toy bow and arrow chasing them. I could see the event in my mind and I couldn't help but laugh, but then I wondered how many Christians are like that procession when it comes to confronting Satan?

The Bible tells us to be sober when it comes to our adversary the devil, for he is a roaring lion looking to see who he can devour, but how many are treating the enemy as if he is no real threat and the spiritual battle as if it is some game (*1 Peter 5:8-10*)? They put on an imaginary armor and wield the Bible like a paper sword because they don't believe it and have no clue as to how they would use it if it was real to them. The turkeys and dog were running away out of fear from someone who did not have any means to really harm them.

As believers, how many of us are running from the enemy out of fear rather than turning and facing him with the authority allotted us to stand, the power of the Spirit to withstand, and with the sword of the Word raised up to continue to stand, knowing the battle belongs to the Lord and that the Word will cause Satan to eventually flee (*1 Samuel 17:45-50; 2 Chronicles 20:15; 2 Timothy 1:7; James 4:7*)?

I often tell people that ministry is all about deliverance but the real deliverance comes when people humble themselves before God who is the sole deliverer and believe His Word, which is the sole spiritual weapon that can push Satan back in his attacks and plans. As we often quote without understanding it, *"And ye shall know the truth, and the truth shall make you free"* (*John 8:32*). (RK)

6) The greatest battle is in the mind. Paul makes it clear that the strongholds are in the mind and these make up the imaginations that exalt themselves against the true knowledge of God (*2 Corinthians 10:3-5*). The Holy Spirit will speak to our spirit and not our mind. As soon as a person goes into the mind to understand the unseen world, the Holy Spirit

will be silent. Fear is one of the more predominate spirits in operation in the world, the mind is often the altar of idolatry that erects a god to its own liking, unbelief serves as a foundation to ignorance, and the rebellion of sin in any form serves as an open invitation for Satan to come in and do his bidding.

Chapter 3: Curses, Are They Real?

1) Curses are a form of witchcraft that set up an environment that is conducive to its claims. According to Strong's Concordance, such words as "swift, small, to somewhat move and to abate, make contempt" are associated with curse. (Hebrew #7043). For example, I have seen the abominable sin of molestation passed down from generation to generation, setting up an environment of shame, unspeakable assault against innocence, and the grave darkness of silence covering up abomination. Like Cain, curses mark people and it seems that the predators of this world can see certain marks, causing the innocent to fall prey to their sin. Until the curse is broken and the mark done away with by the blood of Jesus, it seems to continue plaguing that particular group or family.

Example: A mother came to me who had two sons in great bondage. As we prayed about it, we encountered a claim put on them by their father's religious cult. Claims often turn into curses because if you fail to do the bidding of that which claims you for its own purposes, bad things (curses) will happen. This is where superstition, fear, guilt, and condemnation can play a big part in the lives of people who have not been set free by the truth of God's Word. These boys were both under the claim that had turned into curses. Both the claim and the curses were broken and her sons became what some would refer to as being "normal." Jesus became a curse for us on the cross so we do not have to accept any cursed existence and if we are believers, we belong to Jesus and no one else has any claims or rights to us (*1 Corinthians 6:18-20; 7:22-24; Galatians 3:13*). (RK)

2) Curses are based on lies, generational sins, and powerful incantations. There are generational curses and word curses. As stated, curses can be passed from generation to generation until they are brought to the light by the Lord and broken. But there are people, like witches or those in a wrong spirit, that can send word curses that will also set up an environment as well. Curses can be easily discerned and easily broken. Life happens, but Satan often overplays his hand and his works of darkness become a bit too much in the way things happen to the point it seems utterly ridiculous, and obvious that the kingdom of darkness is behind it.

Example: A certain young East Indian woman from South Africa who was well indoctrinated into witchcraft, curses, and so forth moved to America and married a young man we knew. She claimed that she was a Christian, so at first, we welcomed her with open arms, but in a short time, we discerned that she was hiding evil intent and had a lying spirit, among other things. She even bragged a little about her magical powers. When she began to realize that we discerned her true state, and knew some of the underhanded things she was doing, she began sending strong curses and psychic prayer at us, and especially me. As the intensity of her attacks increased, one morning when I was in the shower, a powerful force came against my head in such a way that I knew it was her that had sent it. I suppose you could say that at that point I had "had it!" Enough is enough. I sent it back to her in the name of Jesus and commanded it to all go and never return. I can't remember all I said in spiritual warfare that day, but it was the last attack of its kind from her to come my way. (JH)

3) Satan must have some kind of inroad, avenue or open door before he can enter. Curses, claims and soul ties serve as avenues, while doors are represented by sins such as pride, anger, fornication, idolatry, pornography, drugs (altered state of consciousness), the occult, and error. Spirits can move at will when these inroads are present. They also hide and wait for the right environment to cause some type of chaos, confusion, trauma or depression, and it happens when our guard is down due to such things as challenges, obstacles, sickness, unforgiveness, bitterness, and despair.

Chapter 4: Soul Ties

1) Christians who find themselves entangled in a soul tie know something is not right, but in their examination of the situation they know they did not start out wrong and so they chide themselves as to how did an innocent relationship become controlling or obsessive. They don't realize that there are seducing and lustful spirits in operation. The seducing spirits seduce you into another reality in order to condition or indoctrinate you into giving way to the designs of Satan that will rob you of authority, kill the validity of your testimony, and destroy the life you have in Christ. The lustful spirits magnify something in order to take one's affection captive. What started out as innocent is now entangled into a spiderweb of

confusion, a tormenting whirlpool that constantly leaves you helpless to know what to do about it, and a despairing pit that eventually you realize only God can deliver you from. (*John 10:10; Colossians 3:2; 1 Timothy 4:1-2*).

Example: Many years ago, I had such a strong soul tie with a certain, beguiling individual that when it was finally handed over to the Lord to get rid of, it took an entire day of literally "listening to" and "hearing" its roots being chopped up and dug out of my soul. It was a miserable experience I will never forget. (JH)

2) Soul ties are like ropes or bungie cords that keep pulling you back to a relationship or events, but they also can have roots on them that go into the emotional arena of your soul. Since these ties operate in darkness the light must expose them. However, we have discovered that soul ties that are like ropes and bungie cords can easily enough be cut, but those who have roots to them must be pulled because they can be easily reconnected. When these ties go into the emotional arena, one can feel the tearing, the pulling, and the ripping of them when the Lord begins to pull them out, but in the end, they also feel clean and free (*Matthew 3:10*).

Example: I found myself in a relationship that became confusing to me. Even though things started out innocently enough, it became obvious down the line that things were not right, but I could never put my finger on it. I sensed that my friend had her own struggles with the relationship as well. It was too stifling for both of us, as it harbored silent demands, expectations, and responses, proving to be oppressive.

One night I found myself on the floor crying out to God because I knew there were things that were wrong in my life. The main fruit of my spiritual existence was the joy of my salvation but it was missing and I cried out for His mercy. For the next two hours the Lord gently dealt with me over various things that consisted of many "little foxes" destroying the vine of fellowship with Him, but I knew things were changing inside. There seemed to be ripping, tearing, and pulling. When it was over, I got up feeling cleansed and revived with a new perspective and the joy of my salvation was once again restored to me.

Things had definitely changed and one of the casualties was my friendship with this person. What God has put together, no man must tear asunder, but what God divides and separates, no man must try to put it back together. It was not until I met Jeannette that I understood what went wrong in my relationship with my friend. Unbeknown to both of us, a soul tie had developed between us, because in the beginning we did enjoy our initial friendship and fellowship. Since neither of us understood the problem, we were unable to discern and didn't understand the spiritual implications behind our struggles and the steps necessary to destroy the works of Satan. (RK)

3) Satan counterfeits everything. God desires souls to be knitted together in agreement to become one in spirit and purpose, but Satan wants to defile that which is pure and righteous, and hence enters in soul ties that become a form of witchcraft to profane and oppress through lusts, control, and obsession. The Holy Spirit gives us valuable insight in order to minister, but through religious and familiar spirits the enemy of our soul impersonates the work of the Holy Spirit in order to sow seeds of religious pride, judgmentalism, and discord. God has given

us prophecy, but Satan has given us different forms of false divination such as astrology for example. It is for this reason we must discern the spirit to make sure we are not missing what is excellent and test the spirits to make sure we are not partaking of the poisonous fruit of this age.

Example: This event actually took place. Back in the early 1980's I was exhibiting my paintings at a certain mall along with other artists. Most of us were staying in our RV's in a back section of the large parking lot for the weekend. I was looking forward to time alone to rest, read and relax in spite of all the noise coming from the RV parked next to mine. It seemed as if all the other exhibiters, none of which I knew, were having a great time. Little did I know that God was going to show Himself mighty, and perform a miracle I will never forget.

The woman who owned said RV suddenly rapped on the door. I opened it and she insisted that I join them. I politely told her "Thanks, but no thanks"; however, she was so persistent that I relented and followed her. Once inside, I made my way through a group of animated people and tried to become inconspicuous in a corner. But, it's impossible to be inconspicuous in a small space.

What the excitement was all about was the woman who owned the RV was reading cards for everyone, and people were talking excitedly about how "right on" she was, and how could she "know all about them." Before I could figure out how to squeeze out of there, she called me up to the table to have my cards read.

Praying inwardly, I heard myself say to her, "No thanks. It won't work for me." "Of course, it will," she said and insisted I come sit down and cut the cards, which I did, and turned up a Jack. I didn't know what to expect, and was surprised when she

110

snatched the card up, and said, "Cut the cards again" and it was another Jack. Somewhat miffed, she said, "Take the card off the top." Well, that card was a Jack too, and I could see she was getting visibly nervous. An uncomfortable hush had fallen over the group who, by now, were focused on what was taking place. Tersely she ordered, "Take the card off the bottom." I did so, and guess what it was? A Jack! Visibly shaken, she dropped the cards and said, "Let's all go out to dinner!" Not one person spoke one word to me that night, or, as far as I can remember, for the rest of the weekend.

The next Sunday in church, I told of this strange event and one of the men explained to me that the Jack is the only card a Medium can't "read" because it stands for Jesus Christ! How great is our God! (JH)

4) It is one thing to unknowingly walk into the camp of Satan. The Lord protects such people, but to walk knowingly into the camp of Satan with the idea that you can't be harmed is arrogance and foolishness. It is important to realize that you will be spiritually exposing yourself to wrong spirits and they are greater than the flesh you are operating in. If God does not call you into the enemy's camp for the purpose of warning or contending for the souls of possible heirs, you have no business exposing yourself in such a way. The Bible clearly commands us in *2 Corinthians 6:14-18* to come out and be separate from all such influences and agreement because the two will never mix (*Amos 3:3; 2 Corinthians 3:5*).

Example: I knew a minister whose call was to pass out tracks about God's good news. He would go into the bars that he was well acquainted with from his past and talk to the patrons and leave tracks. This man had a calling and the influences around him had no real attraction to him.

However, I had a friend who tried to talk me into going to a New Age retreat with her that was being sponsored by her relative's church. She wanted to protect this relative from being influenced by the anti-Christ spirit that would be present. I turned her down and she went knowing that the spirit was wrong. Her attitude was that since she was aware of it, it would not hurt her. The attitude she possessed was the pride of self-sufficiency and the flesh was an open door to the wiles of Satan. When she came back her eyes mirrored the glint of a false light, her attitude was changed and our relationship greatly changed as well. (RK)

Chapter 5: Psychic Prayer

1) Satan is the prince of the power of the air (*Ephesians 2:2*). Air has to do with breath and it takes breath to speak. Incense symbolizes how prayers will go up through the air and space. Satan governs the territory between heaven and earth and is the god of the systems of the world, where he exerts unseen power (*2 Corinthians 4:3-4*). Since he is the prince of the air all prayers go through his realm and if they are not in line with God's will, he can use them as he sees fit.

Psychic prayers are a form of witchcraft because they often collide with the person's will who is on the receiving end, sometimes causing mental challenges. They also are sent to cause problems.

Example: The Lord sent us into a small country church a number of years ago. The pastor was young and had a family, but something was terribly wrong. His wife was totally oppressed, for one thing, and his short sermons never coincided or incorporated any of the scriptures he read at the beginning of a service. There was no anointing on him at all, and he seemed nervous and angry most of the time; but what really gave him away were his eyes because they were the cold, hard, dark eyes of a warlock. His demons knew I knew what he was (our ministry team all did) but he singled me out for powerful psychic attacks, especially at night when he worked his night job. One night, while asleep, I experienced demons with long claws grabbing at my legs, trying to drag me down into hell while he watched from a distance. Apparently, I was screaming in terror so loud that I awoke Rayola who came to see what was going on. Surprised that I was fast asleep, she woke me up and after hearing what I was experiencing, she prayed for me. I had other attacks, but praise the LORD, He always showed me what he was up to and what he was planning to do. It was a harrowing few months of unforgettable, relentless and intense spiritual warfare, fighting against familiar spirits, curses, and psychic attacks, plus slander, but the Holy Spirit won, he was expelled and later moved to another state. (JH)

2) Psychic prayer can become a demonic covering that will cause confusion and make a person feel as if they are walking in mud. In essence, they are hitting the covering (Isaiah 25:7).
3) Some Christians do not understand the spiritual realm so when they pray their will on something that is not in line with God's will, Satan can use that against the one their prayers are directed at, but there are those who exert psychic prayer to get others to see it their way or do their bidding. When it comes to dealing with psychic prayer, one needs to discern where it is coming from. If it is coming from someone who is ignorant about such matters, I ask the Lord to let it fall to the

wayside, but if it is a source of witchcraft, I ask the Lord to send it back to the source.

Example: One summer there were some incidents that happened to us that we knew were sent through psychic attacks from a certain woman who had been conniving for years to acquire my inheritance as the only heir to a substantial amount. About the time she would've received an Affidavit from me contesting the Will because of several illegal, immoral and fraudulent maneuvers she had made to secure it, our yard was targeted out of the entire neighborhood by a microburst that flung our patio umbrella over a 6' fence and slammed it against a neighbor's house, destroying the umbrella completely. At the same time, it actually bent our Valley Forge, American made, 20' tall flag pole. And the worst thing that happened is the torn ligament that Rayola suffered from merely stepping up onto the back step! (As of this writing, there is no conclusion to the legal matter which did not involve money, but required only certain moral actions on her part.) (JH)

4) There are those who unknowingly come into agreement with psychic prayer because they do not know how to discern the spirit behind a person. People who deal in this type of witchcraft want to be spiritual bigshots. They will take on the causes of others in order to impress them by agreeing to pray with them about a matter. This agreement can be powerful as well as dangerous to the one the prayers are directed at if they are not able to discern what is going on.

Example: I was aware that a particular individual (referred to as A) wanted me to perform a certain way to make her feel better about her world and her relationship with me. I had to push aside her prayers that Satan slammed against me at different times. One day this woman found someone (we'll call B) who sided with her and prayed that A's will and desire be done where I was concerned. This individual wanted to impress A with how Christian and spiritual she was. One day I was at the gym and was ready to enter the pool area. I stepped into a small puddle of water and went face down on the cement floor. I ended up with a slight concussion that caused my mind to be befuddled, as well as pushed my nose back so that it had to be adjusted, and sprang my foot.

I was visiting with A when the other individual joined us. As I was relating to A about my accident, I looked over to B and she had a slight smile on her face and a smug look to go along with it. I then realized it was psychic prayer and that in spite of it, God had protected me because it could have been much worse, and at that time I became aware that I indeed had a foe. (RK)

Chapter 6: Can Christians Be Possessed?

1) Man is made up of spirit, soul, and body (*1 Thessalonians 5:23*). The spirit is considered the higher estate of man because only spirit can affect it, while the soul is considered the lower state of man because it is affected by both the spirits of the unseen world and the material world around it.

2) If a person is born again, the demonic realm can't take possession of the person's spirit, but the soul that is made up of the will, mind and emotions can be oppressed by the demonic realm because the three arenas of the soul, (flesh, eyes, and pride) is where the avenues and doors exist that open the way for oppression to take place (*1 John 2:15-17*).

And, when the oppression is exposed, the demonic world will manifest itself through the body.

Example of demonic manifestations: Sometimes when a Christian has unwittingly opened a door to a demonic entity, or spirit of fear, lying spirit, unclean spirit, mocking spirit, or spirit of lust, etc. they may manifest in your presence when you go to pray for them. Usually, such manifestations take the form of uncontrollable shaking or trembling, and sometimes they will even cry out, or even spit at you, threaten to hit you, or tear things apart. We have encountered all of these things through the years. (JH)

3. Satan lies in wait. The oppression I have encountered in the lives of Christians is often the result of past events that have been misconstrued in the tender mind of youth, hidden in some type of darkness of shame, or resulted in a bad determination. Only the light of God can expose such bondages. Even though we are born again, those places can remain intact until the fruits make it obvious that something is not quite right and we turn to the great Physician for healing (*Luke 4:18-19*). At such times we learn what it means to stand by faith, withstand with truth, and continue to stand in light of the heavenly.

Once we come out on the other end of our process, we can enter the ministry of consolation and reconciliation (*2 Corinthians 1:3-7; 5:18-20*). We now have the ability to enter in with the hurting, wounded, and downcast as we take their hand and lead them through demonic valleys of humiliation into His healing light. Remember, we can only lead people where we have already been.

Examples: What many Christians don't understand is that God uses Satan and his realm to test, prepare, and season His servants. Peter was sifted by Satan so he would be converted, Job was refined in the ovens so he could come forth as gold, and Paul had a thorn in his side so that he would not become lifted up. He needed to remember that it is God's grace that proves to be sufficient during troubling and challenging times (*Job 23:10; Luke 22:31-32; 2 Corinthians 12:2-10*). I have learned to be a seasoned minister through testing, an effective soldier in battle, and an overcomer in obedience to God's Word. Jesus said we would have much tribulation in the world in *John 16:33*. In *Acts 14:22* we are told that we enter the kingdom of heaven through much tribulation.

Chapter 7: Familiar Spirits

1) Familiar spirits are all around us, spying and seeking information. Our friend, who was well-acquainted with witchcraft and was delivered out of it, came into our house, looked around, and admitted there were no "swirlies" hovering in our home. I asked her what they were and she stated, "familiar spirits."

Example: Years ago, when I was a young, enthusiastic woman, and before the Lord called me into full-time ministry, I had an experience that taught me how very real familiar spirits are. I was alone in my kitchen talking to the Lord about my heart desire to serve Him. I mentioned a certain very famous woman evangelist (by then deceased) as an example of the kind of minister I would like to be. I had never mentioned that woman's name to anyone, and certainly never disclosed to a living soul what I had prayed in the privacy of my home; but later in the afternoon a friend, who lived many miles from me, called on the phone to talk and what she said chilled me to the bone. She quoted back to me the words that I had prayed to the Lord, even to mentioning the name of the person I had spoken to the Lord about. Then she proceeded to tell me what I had to do to "have a ministry" like that woman! How could she have so precisely known all that? The answer is, a familiar spirit told her. (JH)

2) Familiar spirits can give details about other people that are "none of their business" in order to cause discord, division or delusion. This is how witches and others in the occult gain private information. Christians need to discern if what they suddenly "hear" is from a familiar spirit or the Holy Spirit. The Holy Spirit never gives details about sins and destructive events. He gives impressions as to how something affects a person so that you can minister to them. However, familiar spirits give details that can hurt someone and haunt you, as well as unknown information that is able to cause discord. In fact, demons like the spotlight and such works such as *A Course in Miracles* are channeled, demonic ramblings.

Example: One time Rayola and I were discussing at home, by ourselves, spiritual matters such as what was lacking in the church and what we could add to our Bible study, and so forth. I can't recall what one of the statements was that we made, but the next time we saw the pastor's wife, she spoke up and quoted that particular statement, word for word! We were astonished, and then realized that a familiar spirit told her what we had said. (JH)

3) Since a familiar spirit talks about people and events, it is often mistaken for the Holy Spirit. However, the type of information that is given along with the type of environment it sets up will clearly identify what spirit is behind the information. If it is not Scriptural, and is not given discreetly to ensure that the environment and people involved are not profaned in any way, then you know that it is not the Holy Spirit.

Chapter 8: Religious Spirits

1. Satan is very religious. He can come as an angel of light and his servants as ministers of righteousness. He can seduce with false light, beguile with cunning expertise, and ensnare with false promises. The truth is Satan not only can counterfeit religion and quote Scripture (out of context as he did to Jesus in the wilderness), but he makes it attractive. Such religion often appeals to the flesh as to the type of experience that it can produce, the pride of life that entails elitism, and having something of worth that will make the person stand out (*2 Corinthians 11:2-15*).

Example: One Sunday in a certain church the Lord had us attend for a short time, there was a young man in whom we had discerned a religious spirit. This particular day he was sitting on the other side of the center aisle from us, and he began talking out loud and mumbled comments through the entire sermon. This was, of course, a great disturbance to the preacher. At the close of his sermon, this young man stood up and made his way across the church to another young man who was sitting directly in front of us and he suddenly laid hands on him and began praying. The whole thing was out of order. As people began to leave, we confronted this young man and told him he had a religious spirit, and that he was out of order according to Scripture. He refused to come clean of it. (JH)

2) People open themselves up to a religious spirit because they want to appear spiritual, and be important, and noticed, but they lack the goods. They want the notoriety without the price that comes along with knowing God in a personal way. They want to run and not wait, jump to the "head of the table" instead of being content to sit in the lowest seat and simply learn of Jesus. People who have such a spirit want to be seen, standing in front touting their spirituality, and be recognized as the one to come to for a word, prayer, or laying on of hands.

Example: We were at a church to hear Betty Swinford speak. It was time for prayer and that is when religious spirits will manifest themselves. A man was standing in front of us and began to sway back and forth while repeatedly saying, "I will serve You, Jesus." We watched him work himself up to where his swaying was becoming more erratic and his declaration louder.

Eventually, the religious spirit picked him up and flung him to the floor and he ended up hitting the pew and flying sideways against the wall. A young pastor misread the happening as being of the Holy Spirit and prayed that the Holy Spirit would continue to minister to this man. The man eventually got up with a bump and cut on his head. The next night Betty Swinford spoke on religious spirits, giving them notice, and that night they were silent and there was order in the meeting. (RK)

Chapter 9: White Witchcraft in Churches

1) It is hard to imagine that there is white witchcraft in churches. There is no such thing as "white" or "acceptable" witchcraft. We knew an oppressed lady who viciously came against us because we believed what scripture said about the Lordship of Jesus. We later learned that she dabbled in so-called "Christian astrology." Anything that is attached to the demonic world is all darkness because it is about rebellion, control and getting one's way. Satan and his demons love high places where they receive attention and adoration. Therefore, it is not unusual to see people in leadership positions in churches that operate with familiar spirits, religious spirits, and beguiling spirits.

Example: We were attending a church where there was a woman who was considered a prophetess. To Jeannette and myself she looked like a former convict, but it was clear she thought of herself as a big shot and sadly those around her treated her as one. However, she and her preacher husband, who was the assistant pastor, were in error. One morning they had missionaries from the Philippines attending the church. They were friends of this heretical couple, but they seemed to have a real heart towards God.

My prayer was simple and I said it in my mind, "Lord cause these missionaries to see the error of this woman and her husband so they might be able to challenge them with Your Word of truth." Keep in mind, I only said this in my mind, but after it was done, the false prophetess looked straight at me with glaring anger and even went over to the head pastor and interrupted his talk to tell him what her familiar spirit had revealed to her. As the pastor listened to her, he even looked at me. Even though the silent prayer was only in my mind, the familiar spirit heard it and told her his perverted version of it. (RK)

2) The most popular power plays that take place in churches happen in the music department. If you are in music, you are assured of a place to stand up in front where you will be recognized. The temptation for religious spirits is that they need to be recognized. We can't begin to tell you the extent of conflicts that take place in the music department that often involves, not only religious spirits, but also the natural spirit that comprises ego, competition, and jealousy.

Example: We had pastor friends that told us about an incident in their church. The pastor and his wife were "straight arrows" as far as the Word of God. A music pastor joined the team at church but after a while they could tell he perceived himself to be a better pastor. He began to try to secure a following in order to take over the church.

In church one Sunday, he stood up in the loft and began to yell out a correction to the pastor concerning his message. Our pastor friend, right then from the pulpit, pointed his finger at the wolf and rebuked him in the name of Jesus. The imposter fell to the floor, unresponsive.

When he finally came to, our friends tried to contend with him but he would have none of it. He left the church to never return.

Chapter 10: The Laying on of Hands

1) In the Old Testament they lay hands on the kings, priests, and prophets to ordain them and the sacrifices to designate them. It was not only a point of identification and consecration, but anointing and calling. It is also a one of the six principle doctrines of Christ carried forward from the Old Testament into the New Testament (*Hebrews 6:1-2*).

Example: I am told that in the church of China when one is called out as a missionary to other places, the elders anoint them, send them forth with some aid to help them fulfill their calling and mission. The reason they do this is because it is a scriptural responsibility to do so. (RK)

2) It is important to note that even witches and new agers transfer spirits by the laying on of hands. When I go to lay hands on someone, I first discern if that is what the Lord wants and then I ask the person if I can lay hands on them. When we let someone lay hands on us, we are opening ourselves up to receive what they have to impart.

Example: This practice of laying on of hands is a serious matter and must not be taken lightly. Even holding hands in a religious environment can cause you to be susceptible to a wrong spirit. In two incidents of taking one's hand, one at church, the other at a dinner table, I felt an unclean spirit climb up my arm. It left a sensation as if there was acid of some type burning my arm. For that reason, I avoid holding hands with someone who may have a wrong spirit until I can discern otherwise. (RK)

A close friend of mine, along with her husband (both Christians) and their two sons, lived on an Indian reservation in Washington state. Her oldest son was maybe in his early teens when a close friend of his, who was involved in some of the native tribal spirituality, told him that he wanted him to have the "same spirit" that he had. He then proceeded to lay hands on her son. Whatever spirit he imparted did indeed enter the young man. His alarmed mother said that his behavior and attitudes were instantly altered in a bad way and remained so until she and her husband confronted it.

Another graphic, and tragic, example of the wrong laying on of hands took place when a close friend of ours (whose encouragement for our ministry, and bubbling enthusiasm for the Lord was always uplifting) decided to travel from her home in Arizona to Florida where she attended a "revival" in a mega church. There she received the laying on of hands by the leader himself, but what was imparted to her was not of God, but instead was one of the most deceiving, malicious and lying spirits we've encountered. This powerful lying spirit began "showing" her horrible, wicked and evil imaginings against myself, and later the same lies about another precious sister in the Lord. She refused any Scriptural correction or instruction to the contrary, and as far as we know, she never repented of it nor was set free. (JH)

3) We are not to let any person suddenly lay hands on us because a wrong spirit can take hold of us (*1 Timothy 5:22*). Regardless of their status, we must discern those who lay hands on us and take authority when necessary to resist Satan's overtures to attach something to us.

Example: A missionary to India came to see us. He was having spiritual struggles, the most serious problem being that he no longer had any desire to read the Word and when he did, it did not have any impact on him. This was not always so, and he knew that without the sword of the Word of God he would not survive on the mission field.

When questioning him about when he lost his love for the Word, he related how a famous heretic's wife laid hands on him. He immediately felt like lust was besieging him and he lost a desire for the Word of God.

We laid hands on him and reversed the covering and claims of the wrong laying of hands. He walked away cleansed and free to once again enjoy God's precious Word. (RK)

Chapter 11: Four Striking Levels

1) We must discern depression. It can be physical, emotional or spiritual. Physical depression has to do with health, and the emotional with loss or crises, but the spiritual has to do with the demonic world. We will naturally encounter the first two types of depression because life happens. When it comes to the physical arena we must cling to the Lord and His Word, and when it comes to the emotional, we must walk through it by faith holding His hand. However, when the dark demonic covering of depression envelops us, we must discern it and take authority over it.

Example: Not all people feel depression and don't always recognize the fruits of it. There was a time when I was irritable, contending with mood swings, and caught off guard by my emotional reaction to things. I struggled in prayer as to what was going on and finally, I asked the Lord about it. He showed me I was depressed due to the various physical problems I was having that were affecting my liver and my emotional well-being. He showed me I was not to be hard on myself, but that I could not give in to any emotional habits as I patiently walked through it. (RK)

2) Oppression points to some form of attack or opening in the soul area where the kingdom of darkness is present and operating. It often manifests itself in depression that could include despair, frustration, anger, and hopelessness. Since the works of the demonic world are founded on lies and hidden under darkness, it is hard to discern where it is coming from. It can become what we consider to be a usual part of the landscape of our soul. It may seem natural, normal, and just part of life, and something we will have to live with. However, when Satan overplays his hand, the demonic oppression becomes obvious. We must seek the light of God to penetrate such darkness in order to address the oppression and take authority over it.

Example: One morning, years ago, after I got out of bed and headed to the bathroom I was just fine. However, once I got there, I was instantly struck with what I refer to as "a sickness unto death." I had never been suddenly hit with anything like it before (or since) and I knew it was a direct attack of Satan.

I was so violently sick I couldn't even open my mouth to speak the Name of Jesus, but in my mind, I cried out to God, and instantly, just as quickly as it had come, it left! This may leave you wondering if the enemy can know our thoughts. As for me, I believe he can. I've heard his celestial, yet evil, voice speak into my mind as well. That incident occurred after I experienced a crushing betrayal that left me so utterly devastated that I wept day and night for about two weeks. As I was just beginning to regain my emotional and spiritual footing, suddenly a very celestially-toned voice clearly said to me, "I can kill you."

I was stunned for a few seconds, and then recognized that I had just heard the voice of Lucifer, the fallen angel himself, and that underneath that suave tone it actually seethed with an evil so deep no one could find a bottom to it. I realized that, yes, he *could* kill me IF I gave in to fear and the terrible emotional pit I was climbing out of and killed myself. So, what he said was a half-truth. As my mind processed all this, his presence remained as if waiting to "help" me put an end to my misery. Then the Holy Spirit rose up within me and I loudly commanded, "Satan, In the Name of Jesus GO! GET OUT OF THIS HOUSE! NOW!" With that, he quickly departed. Praise the Lord! (JH)

3) The people that come under demonic influences such as seduction and lust find themselves often being driven by obsessions that find their springboard in lust that has quickly taken their imagination or affections captive. Whether it is based on possibilities of ecstasy, tormenting addictions, or unabated desire to taste whatever fruit has captured its attention, demonic obsessions declare the person must take possession of the fruit regardless of right or wrong. They MUST taste of it, for it to be satisfied and the obsession stopped. However, if such people finally do taste the fruit, it often turns into contempt because it didn't meet their expectations, or it left them feeling hollow, guilty and condemned. Obsessions are insatiable appetites that can

drive a person to the point of insanity, where reason, consequences, and results are missing from the equation.

Example: Many years ago, a friend and I went to a certain big church to hear a vocalist. He was young, handsome and definitely talented; but I discerned a huge spirit of lust, and also a powerful beguiling spirit that seemed to be flowing over the entire church. Much to my dismay, my friend was so enraptured by him that she insisted we come back to his second performance; however, after she realized what was happening to her, she agreed that he had a powerful seductive spirit and we stayed away. (JH)

4) The word, "possession" explains it all. The person is possessed in the spirit by demons, driven in the soul by them, and this possession will clearly manifest itself in the body, especially when the presence of God is present. One might ask how can a person give way to possession knowing the end results?

It is important to understand that demon possession is a result of two wrong choices. First, demonic entities give their hosts power. They are constant companions and quite entertaining, but they are also tormenting. When people come to us, they often come seeking relief from the torment, but not deliverance from the demonic power.

When people come merely seeking relief, they rob you of your time, make a mockery out of your attempts, and walk away just as oppressed and possessed as before. Since they prefer the power of darkness, they will not humble themselves and turn to God in repentance and choose to believe Him and prefer His Word. God's Word is what will cut away all oppression and bring a defeating blow to possession.

The second choice comes down to lordship. Who will be lord of your life: Satan or Jesus. Lordship points to ownership. Owners are the ones who give servants the type of authority they are to operate in and the service they are to render according to their calling.

Possessed people have, somewhere along the line, submitted to the lordship of Satan. For them to be totally delivered from his claims and rights on their life, they must turn from the darkness and totally surrender to the Lord of lords, Jesus Christ.

Example: Jeannette looked at the woman sitting in a chair a few feet away from her. She stated, "You are a witch aren't you." The lady looked at her with a smug smile as if to say, "You finally got it."

This woman had called our office after we had been on the radio promoting our first book. A caller had asked about deliverance. The question had caught this woman's attention and she called asking for an appointment. When she arrived at our office, I asked her what her problem was and she stated, "I have demons and they're tormenting me."

When people say they have demons, I would suggest that you refrain from smiling, and take them seriously. I have yet to meet one person who has stated that they had this problem who didn't. At times the declarations can be exaggerated, arrogant, and ridiculous, but nevertheless, there is truth in it.

It was obvious this woman was possessed. After five hours of casting our demons, encountering various manifestations, we managed to get down to the person. At that time the Lord revealed to Jeannette that she was a witch. When questioned, she admitted that she had married Satan. When asked why she went to the side of darkness, she said she was just living her life when through some religious encounter the truth of God and hell intruded into her reality. She became angry that there was some God who would cast her into hell because she didn't do it His way. She then turned to the side of darkness and embraced it since she could pretty well live as she so desired.

She told us for the most part her demons gave her power and entertained her, but they also tormented her. She had gone to various churches and went forward to get "saved," without any results. She left me wondering as to how many witches sit in our churches, cursing, mocking, and playing some sick little game without even being discerned.

We had two other sessions with her. In the second one the demons were back and we realized she was robbing us of our time. The third time I began to speak of her sin and her demons closed her down for about 20 minutes. Once she came out of it, she left.

Through it all she was clearly operating in her witchcraft. I had experienced an attack from her while going into a store. It felt like an ax hit me in the back and I almost went to the floor. A quick rebuke caused it to lift. Jeannette sensed her presence in our condo one night. It was clear she could astral-project. She demanded that it be gone in the name of Jesus and it had to go.

We invited her to go to church. Our pastor did discern her demonic presence and rebuked it. The next Sunday he was deathly sick and knew it was demonic and where it came from.

The Sunday the main pastor was sick, the assistant pastor basically "entertained" us with his wit and charm. The witch enjoyed him and it was obvious he posed no threat to her demons.

The final time I saw her was at church on Resurrection Sunday. The pastor preached a great sermon on Lordship. She came up and told me she was ready to be delivered. I looked at this possessed woman who was a game player and time-robber and told her, "I can cast demons out of you in the name of Jesus, but if you want to be delivered, you have to change your lord from Satan to Jesus. If you don't change your master, there is nothing more I can do for you."

She walked away. Later she called me for my advice as to how she could deliver herself. I told her I could give her no other advice, and that was the last I heard from her. (RK)

WORD OF KNOWLEDGE

BY

BETTY SWINFORD

First Edition 1976

Word of Knowledge

Copyright © 1976 by Betty Swinford

Second reprint 2023 by Gentle Shepherd Ministries.

Hidden Manna Publications
P.O. Box 3572
Oldtown, ID 83822
www.gentleshepherd.com

Facebook:
https://www.facebook.com/HiddenMannaPublications/

CONTENTS

FORWARD

The deep, life-transforming teaching of Evangelist Betty Swinford on the Word of God some four years ago at a Charismatic meeting in Modesto, California affected my spirit intensely. I became open and yielded for all that God wanted to manifest to and through me by His Holy Spirit.

I had seen the gift of the word of knowledge powerfully used in various Kathryn Khulman services throughout California prior to Mrs. Swinford's coming to Modesto in 1972. However, as Betty Swinford conducted the services, I was to personally experience the glorious power of God — both in healing and in falling under the power.

The first service I attended there was such singing in the Spirit that we were all caught up into the presence Of God. One young man sang a message in tongues, and the interpretation followed also in song. *"Oh, Thou magnificent One who sitteth upon the throne; to Thee do we give all honor and praise!"* What an intense knowing that the Holy Spirit was in that place! His presence was simply breathtaking, intangible yet so real that one felt saturated, permeated by His power.

Earlier that month the doctor had diagnosed, with the help of X-rays, the disease of diverticulitis and diverticulosis. I had been suffering for six months previous to this diagnosis. My doctor put me on a very bland diet in hopes that I would become pain-free and the disease controlled.

However, God is still a God of healing. When Betty called a prayer line, I stepped into it. She reached out, praying, to touch me. Before that touch came, I was under the power and unable to rise to my feet! I felt as though I were basking in the love of God. Quietly, so quietly I heard myself singing praises to Him. (This is not exactly the common thing for a woman who had been the wife of an Episcopal priest for 19 years, but then we are, after all, living in glorious days when God is doing a new thing!)

One evening, as Betty Swinford was calling out some afflictions by the word of knowledge, I saw her coming down the side aisle. I was awed by the power of God and what I had already experienced. Now she drew me from my seat and I told her that God was blessing me so beautifully and that I was experiencing a gradual healing in my body. She replied quietly, "God wants to complete that healing." Before she could touch me, I was under the power again, and when I got back to my feet I was totally healed. That was four years ago this month, and I am still healed, praise God. When He works, it is with such perfection.

One of my friends was called out of her seat by Mrs. Swinford. She was a Southern Baptist, whose need was for healing for her daughter-in-law of a fatal disease. She was slain under the power for 45 minutes, and her son's wife was completely healed.

How the power of the Holy Spirit guided, directed and sovereignly governed those meetings! But you will hear Betty Swinford say it over and over; "I am not God. I cannot heal you. If God doesn't move, if He does not impart knowledge, then nothing is going to happen. I know where it all comes from!

Olivia Williams

Chapter One

BEYOND HUMAN INTELLECT

The auditorium was packed to capacity. The man who stood on the square, raised platform in the middle of the room was handsome, broad-shouldered and charming. He spoke eloquently, disarmingly and quoted Scriptures by the ream. The crowd was totally captivated by his charm, knowledge and dynamic.

I had come to the meeting with my parents from Terre Haute, Indiana to hear this up-and-coming evangelist. His popularity had sprung up almost overnight and was spreading rapidly, especially in our state. People had driven for hundreds of miles to hear him in this afternoon session.

Only a few weeks old in Christ, I was excited and eager to hear everyone, everything. I wanted to know about Jesus Christ, and I had not the faintest idea that anyone could go by the name 'Christian' and be anything but genuine. This was to be my first encounter with such an individual.

Raised in a home where I never went to church except at Easter and Christmas, I was nearly as ignorant of God and His word as an aborigine. I was also ignorant of the Holy Spirit, His work and His gifts. In my intense hunger for reality in life, I had walked the lonely streets of Martinsville, Illinois in the early morning hours, searching, groping. My first meeting with the

Holy Spirit was when He prompted me to cry the anguished words; "Oh, my God, who are You? God, where are You? Is it remotely possible that I could ever know you?"

And because God is who He is, and because He placed that hunger within my heart, He set circumstances into motion to meet and satisfy that hunger. I was converted and soundly so in the First Baptist Church of West Terre Haute, Indiana under the singing ministry of Chief White Feather, grandson of Sitting Bull.

My life was transformed. Not knowing even one verse of Scripture, not knowing a hymn or a chorus and certainly knowing nothing of the work of the Spirit, I was nonetheless taught by Him.

Within twenty-four hours I was very much aware of being a new creature in Christ. Old habits and hangups fell away like filthy rags, without effort or struggle. But I also was aware that now I had an enemy whose territory had been invaded by Christ, when He snatched me from the stronghold and brought me to Himself. I also learned that the spiritual hunger had only been accentuated rather than assuaged. So, I went to church every time a service was in progress, took part in witnessing programs, memorized Scripture verses from the Navigator's Memorization Course and took active part in church visitation.

When the rising young evangelist I spoke of earlier came to our state my parents (who were now really walking with the Lord) decided to go hear him, I went along.

And now, sitting in this crowded auditorium watching the handsome young man on the raised platform, I discovered that I was becoming sick to my stomach. Really sick. And, to make matters worse, the more I listened to this man, the more ill I became.

He was quite dramatic, I remember, but so was Kathryn Kuhlman and she certainly never turned me off! I knew nothing of the anointing of God at that time. But I did know one thing: there had been a very wonderful, intangible something in the ministry of Chief White Feather that had reached the cry of my heart and drawn me to the Saviour. What I sensed in this evangelist was not the same thing, for it turned me away. I wanted only to get out and get away from him.

Words came to my mind. "Phony. He's a phony. Oh God, this man is a phony!'

I was revolted and shocked at my thoughts. Condemnation tumbled in on me. I was accusing a servant of God in being a phony. Not understanding the spiritual gifts or the ways of the Spirit, I tried to talk myself out of what I was feeling. But the word 'phony' stubbornly resisted me.

If there had been struggles against my new enemy before, they were multiplied now. Satan said that I was sinning against God, that my feelings toward this evangelist were my own, and I was grossly filled with guilt.

Yet I knew, and I didn't know how I knew, that what I was seeing, hearing and feeling was bypassing my mind completely. This was beyond human intellect. What I knew was rolling around deep inside of me somewhere, and it was a much greater kind of knowledge than mere human reasoning. I knew. What's more, I knew that I knew. And for some reason, the sickness I felt was a part of it. That man's secret life did not measure up to what he was preaching and I would have staked my life on it. Time would prove it out, and, if the whole world should stand against me, it would make no difference. I knew.

This interior knowledge was mightily reinforced when the evangelist gave the altar call and invited the people to come to himself rather than to Jesus. He prayed after this manner; "Pretty please, Lord Jesus. Come on now, come to. His crooning voice captivated the people and they surged toward the platform in droves, crowding close to be near him.

It seemed to me that his 'ego trip' was too obvious for anyone to miss, but that wasn't the case. And little did I know that what I was experiencing was one of the spiritual gifts.

My parents were planning to give him a sum of money at a later meeting and I thought it was my duty to warn them. But to my astonishment, when I tried to explain to them what I knew to be true, they rose up against me in anger. The evangelist was a man of God. Look at the way he quoted the Word of God! Why, he didn't even open his Bible. I certainly should ask the Lord to forgive me for having such terrible thoughts about a very wonderful man.

Later he came to Terre Haute for a meeting. People stood on solid ice for three hours to get inside the meeting place to hear him. And, because the Word does not return empty, many persons received Christ as Lord and Saviour.

I had tried to share with two friends what I had felt at the first meeting, but their rebukes soon turned me to silence. I no longer tried to tell even my best friends and sought to convince myself that I had been wrong. After all, I reasoned, I had been a new Christian, and others who were wiser and older in Christ than I did not agree with me. They were right, of course. I had been young and zealous — and very, very wrong.

But something bothered me. Condemnation from the devil, rebukes from friends and parents and my own efforts to forget the whole thing did not strike the death blow to that knowledge. It was so deep within that I could not for long be convinced of the man's sincerity. The truth was still there; I had nothing to do with it whatsoever.

Some few years later an article appeared in the newspaper that this same evangelist had raped a seventeen-year-old girl on a train. Later there was more trouble. He set fire to his own church in an attempt to collect insurance. He sent his son into Mexico, where the youth abandoned his father's car, on the pretext that it had been stolen. The father tried again to collect insurance. After that it was a steady stream of troubles. The last thing we heard about him was his arrest in Los Angeles for shoplifting.

I'm not happy that I was right. Besides, it was really the Holy Spirit who was right. He knew all the time that the man was a phony; for it surely takes more than a knowledge of the Bible to make a person sincere in Christ. It took several years, but all that the Lord showed me on that day in Indianapolis came into the light.

I was in the learning process long before I heard of the infilling of the Holy Spirit. These were pre-charismatic days and the gift of the word of knowledge was not flowing in other full-gospel churches as it is today. So, as the Holy Spirit taught me, I learned to remain silent and share with no one, until the proper time came to speak.

Deep, deep in the inner man God speaks, down in the seat of the indwelling Spirit. And when He speaks, you believe. You know. Even if the whole world stands against you, you know. Well-meaning friends and even ministers may tell you it's the 'gift of suspicion', but such folk are spiritually ignorant. They cannot understand, for God in His sovereignty did not choose to give them that particular gift.

The word of knowledge goes beyond human intellect and springs forth from the well of the inner man. First, it is God's knowledge. Then, when it is spoken, it becomes the word of knowledge.

For to one is given, by the Spirit, the word of wisdom; to another, the word of knowledge by the same Spirit; to another, faith by the same Spirit; to another, the gifts of

142

healing by the same Spirit; to another, the working of miracles; to another, prophecy; to another, discerning of spirits; to another, various kinds of tongues; to another, the interpretation of tongues. But all these worketh that one and the very same Spirit, dividing to every man severally as He will (I Corinthians 12:8-11).

Let it be said once and for all that only the spiritual man or woman can truly understand the things of the Spirit. *"For they that are after the flesh do mind the things of the flesh, but they that are after the Spirit, the things of the Spirit" (Romans 8:5).*

Therefore, when I say that the word of knowledge goes beyond human intellect, those of you who are spiritual have already grasped that fact. It's so very simple. The one who is drawn after the Spirit readily understands His ways. Yet for those who have not come this far but who are hungry for the things of the Spirit of God, they will be able to sluff off every shred of immaturity or carnality and be delivered into the 'glorious liberty of the children of God' as you read on.

Chapter Two

WHAT IS IT THEN?

The gift of the word of knowledge was laid on the ecclesiastical shelf for long years. Its flow had begun around the turn of the century when the Holy Spirit was outpoured on hungry groups around the world. The fire of God opened hearts heavenward, the gifts began to operate and the miraculous was breathed around the globe.

But as God moved, Satan counter-moved. Groups of people began forming and moving in questionable directions. Personal prophecy got out of hand. The word of knowledge, instead of being a beautifully shining light, became marred and mixed with human design and purpose. In such a questionable meeting, a man might say either by personal prophecy or the word of knowledge that the pianist was to divorce her husband and marry the minister. And individuals began to misuse God's gifts until those who were truly following the Lord became frightened.

As a result, this precious gift of the word of knowledge was laid on a shelf in most full-gospel circles. Its flow was partially stemmed until the next outpouring which began approximately fifteen years ago, the outpouring which we know to be the charismatic move. With this new deluge of the Holy Spirit, the spiritual gifts began to flow again in a much greater stream. Not only were tongues, interpretation, prophecy, healings and

144

miracles taking place, but all the gifts began to move again. Today I suppose no single gift is talked about more than the gift of the word of knowledge.

What is it? How does it work? When does it work and under what conditions? Who can it move through? (I heard a young convert of five years say the other night: "Not many Christians can handle the word of knowledge. I can handle it. God has trusted me with it.") He said much more than that, but I was too turned off to listen. He was on a real ego trip! The Bible says specifically that the Spirit gives the gifts, *"severally as He will"* (*1 Cor. 12:11*).

The word of knowledge has penetrated deeply into all fellowships and churches where the Spirit of God is free to do His work. Even those who once have now feared or ignored the gift or who at best called it 'suspicion' opened their hearts for the pure, true flow of this gift.

We live in a day when the prophecies of Joel are being fulfilled and when the promises recorded in the book of Isaiah are becoming reality! For God said three times by the prophet Isaiah that He would do a new thing, and He is surely doing just that.

In this wonderful day of change and the Spirit "coming upon all flesh", we see a beautiful restoration to God's people. Long neglected gifts are being restored. No longer are Spirit-filled people afraid of His own works and words. With the operation of the spiritual gifts, there seems to be a greater anointing than ever before.

And what is the gift of the word of knowledge, really? It's a light. A brightly shining light that comes to shine in dark places. It's healing and deliverance and hope and encouragement. It's God the eternal standing beside you saying, "You see? You thought I didn't know what you needed, what you were going through. But I have known all along. And now that I've revealed your need, I'm going to do something about it."

And what is it? A mystical something that comes floating down in a spooky manner to scare people and illuminate their sins? Never! For God does not reveal what has been confessed and forgiven. When it's under the blood, it's gone! Neither does He reveal anything about you in a way that would cause you embarrassment or shame. God just isn't like that.

The word of knowledge *must always be used with discretion.* Otherwise, souls could be irreparably damaged and lives destroyed.

At this writing, I am in a Missouri town holding a meeting. God had shown me the life of a young man at the beginning of the five-night meeting. The knowledge came from deep within, by strong impression. I saw this young man's problem with lust, his violent temper, so violent that at times it took on the propensity of insanity. He could murder when he was that angry. He was trying to fill a place in church leadership, yet he was living a lie.

I prayed earnestly. Twice before in the whole of my ministry I had rebuked individuals openly. "If You would have me call this thing out," I told the Lord, "then Your Spirit will have to so direct me that this man will not be hurt." For I felt strongly that God was going to deal with this particular man publicly.

The confirmation came through his young wife who came to the pastor's home yesterday morning and said; "What . . . . needs is for Betty to stand in the pulpit and say exactly what he is. Then he would accept it."

I had already conferred with the pastor, telling him how I felt the Lord was leading me. (I like for the pastor to know what the Lord is saying — for several reasons. One, he will understand

and be standing with me in prayer. Another reason is that the minister is my point of confirmation. I already know it's accurate, but the Bible still says, *"In the mouth of two or three witnesses every word may be established"* (Matthew 18:16). No evangelist can go wrong by working closely with the pastor and letting him know what you are doing and why.

The building was filled to capacity last night. The service began in an ordinary manner and I was getting ready to lead some choruses, when suddenly the Spirit of God came upon the scene. The word of knowledge began to flow forth, telling of the various hindrances and hangups in this young man's life. It came with such force and such authority that people said later they scarcely dared to breathe. The atmosphere was literally charged with the power of God. The one in question was not identified or called out. Nor indeed should he have been. Yet the Spirit of God so moved upon him that he ran out of his seat and fell at the altar sobbing. He was still there at midnight, praying and seeking the face of God.

This tremendous spiritual gift never hurts; it always heals. And it may be well to remember that what God reveals He is also prepared to heal, whether the thing be in the realm of the physical, mental, emotional or spiritual. Sometimes the Holy Spirit may show the one ministering that there is a deeply painful memory that needs healing. He who knows us so well and loves us so much. He knows exactly what we need and will move heaven and earth in an effort to meet our needs.

You may be thinking; "But how could a person dare to speak, even though he or she was sure it was God showing them something? Can you really be that sure?"

Yes, a person can be that sure. So sure, in fact, that an individual being used in the gift of the word of knowledge would be willing to lay their own life and ministry on the line for this God-given knowledge. And if it was wrong, then it simply was not God.

One knows by impression. By revelation. By feeling the need in his or her own body. Then, when the anointing of authority comes to speak that word, it can only be the proper time and the proper place. The Holy Spirit does the rest.

And suddenly the one the Lord wants to minister to is broken and waiting—and unaware that there is anyone else around in all the world.

What is the word of knowledge? It is truly a light shining down the corridors of life, a light so dazzlingly bright that nothing can escape its beam.

I was weary from ministering in a certain meeting. Some friends asked me to come and spend some time on their farm to rest. I gladly accepted. I stayed in a twenty-eight-foot trailer under a big leafy tree and soaked up the easy life for three beautiful days.

The Taylors had more acreage than I could count. Much of their land was under alfalfa cultivation. A huge modern swather (hay cutter for those of us who aren't too familiar with farm machinery!) with an enclosed cab and large spotlight went out to cut hay at night when it was cool.

I was really enjoying this time of rest. Dressed in old jeans and shirt and tennis shoes, I walked up and down the irrigation ditches picking wild asparagus — which incidentally is fantastic with cream cheese sauce! The smell of horses, hay and pure country air lingered deliciously everywhere. The gentle sounds of rushing water came from a wide irrigation ditch and I sat down on an old unused bridge to dangle my feet in the water.

Marie came to join me and asked if I'd like to ride the hay cutter that night with her son, Eddie. Well, I did want to! My writer's blood surfaced very quickly. New experiences meant new ideas for stories.

At ten o'clock that night I climbed into the high cab with the young man, breathed in the heady fragrance of alfalfa and watched as he switched on the giant floodlight atop the cab. We started out, making a wide, clean path through the field. Then I saw an amazing thing take place. Out of the alfalfa, seconds before those great blades would have cut them to ribbons, darted all manner of little animals. Foxes. Cottontails. Quail and groundhogs. Frightened, they fled for safety.

But it wasn't the cutting blade that sent them charging on their way. It was the great light that ferreted them out of their hiding places. Nothing could escape that gigantic beam of light. It uncovered everything. Except for that light, the creatures would have remained there indefinitely and no one would have guessed that they were nesting and burrowing in the alfalfa.

Now that is what happens when the light of the word of knowledge shines into a person's life. It may be, as we have said, in the area of mind, body, soul or spirit. It may not necessarily be anything wrong in the life at all. There may be a disease, a deep childhood bruising, a mental oppression, an area of fear, a need so deep that it may not have been shared with even a best friend. But our Heavenly Father knows, and what's more important, He cares and understands. He will never reveal a need to hurt, embarrass or otherwise bring even more wounding to an already troubled life. He will only help and heal.

Nothing escapes the light of His knowledge. He knows what lies beyond every façade. He knows all the hindrances that lie hidden within the life. He hears the cry of the heart for release, for freedom.

An incident happened in the meeting tonight that verifies this very fact. A notorious townswoman came to the services for the first time. The people in the church had been praying with some unbelief for this woman. Some admitted that they felt no one could help her, not even God. An alcoholic, it was also evident that she was dealing in prostitution. But. in spite of the unbelief evidenced by some, a Methodist woman took it upon herself to bring this woman to church. She came. Here's what happened.

When I was on the airplane heading for this meeting, the Lord began to show me some of the things I would encounter in the few nights here. One was a woman who took an excessive number of pills. I had not seen her, however, or even felt impressed that she was in any of the services. Until the moment I looked into the face of the alcoholic. I knew she was the one who also took the large amount of pills. Now the Lord said. "Tranquillizers." He did not identify her by being an alcoholic or prostitute, but used the word, tranquillizers.

Would she please identify herself? Her hand shot up. A moment later she came down the aisle for prayer and the next minute she was flat on her back, slain by the power of God. Her face took on the look of an angel. And the peace! It was fathomless. Such a look of rest, inner rest. She later declared by way of testimony. "God did something for me tonight that I've never known before. Oh, do pray for me that I won't go back to the old life."

Paul wrote to the church at Ephesus and said,

That the God of Our Lord Jesus Christ, the Father of glory, may give unto you the spirit of wisdom and

150

revelation in the knowledge of Him. The eyes of your understanding being enlightened, that ye may know what is the hope of your calling, and what the riches of His glory of His inheritance in the saints. And what is the exceeding greatness of His power toward us who believe, according to the working of His mighty power (Ephesians 1:17-20).

The translation in the Living Bible is perhaps even more illuminating, *"asking God, the glorious Father Of our Lord Jesus Christ, to give you wisdom to see clearly and really understand who Christ is and all that He has done for you. I pray that your hearts will be flooded with light so that you can see something of the future He has called you to share."*

And the Amplified says, *"that He may grant you a spirit of wisdom and revelation — of insight into mysteries and secrets — in the (deep and intimate) knowledge of Him, by having the eyes of your heart flooded with light, so that you can know and understand the hope to which He has called you and how rich is His glorious inheritance in the saints — His set-apart ones."*

Yes, the word of knowledge is a light, a beautifully flowing gift that brings hope, peace, healing. It is always coupled with wisdom and discretion or certainly should be. And let us remember that it is no more to God to impart a speck of His knowledge to us than it is for Him to place a language in our mouths that we never learned.

Chapter Three

WHAT IT IS NOT

First of all, the gift of the word of knowledge is not the 'gift of suspicion'. It has already been said that this gift does not operate through 'sense knowledge' or 'common sense knowledge'. But, *"As many as are led by the Spirit of God, they are the sons of God" (Romans 8:14).* And when the Spirit of God places sovereign knowledge within your spirit, the mental or sense knowledge has nothing whatever to do with it.

Yet there are those — even ministers — who deny the usefulness and operation of this spiritual gift and when it begins to move through the life of, perhaps, one of his flock, he feels frightened or threatened. What happens then is a great inner frustration within the life of the one through whose life this gift is beginning to operate.

I have vivid recollections of what I went through after receiving the baptism of the Holy Spirit. Certain spiritual operations began at once in my life. The gift of the word of knowledge, weak and immature, but in definite operation before receiving the fulness of the Spirit, now began to bloom and blossom. But I had had no teaching on it and knew nothing of what to expect, when it should operate or what I should do when God did place His knowledge within me.

It was only natural to go to my pastor and explain my dilemma. To my wondering amazement, he had nothing to say. But on the following prayer meeting night he preached on the gift of 'suspicion'. Needless to say, I was surprised, chagrined and embarrassed. I had gone to him for help and he had rebuked me.

It was hard to understand why the gifts of healing, tongues, interpretation, prophecy and faith could operate in the church, but discerning of spirits and the word of knowledge were strictly taboo. Miracles were permitted but they were scarce.

I stumbled on, groping and praying for understanding. Since the gift was not allowed to operate in the church and since there seemed to be no way of receiving the much longed for teaching, the Lord became my teacher. He put me in kindergarten, and here's how He began.

We were vacationing, on our way to California. Our family was eager to escape the Arizona heat and dip our toes into the icy blue waters of the Pacific Ocean. But in El Centro, which is still a very hot place, our car refrigeration went out. We were left in sweltering heat, without the touch of the icy blue water or even a wonderful first glimpse of it.

My husband took our three children and me to a park and the car to a garage. It took hours to get it fixed and when he came back for us with some soft drinks, we were truly grateful. He had to take the car back to the garage for a final adjustment, then went to pay the bill. I fell into conversation with one of the mechanics.

The man with whom I was speaking commented; "We're getting ready to leave on vacation too. We're planning to go . . ."

In the second he paused, I said as naturally as I could have said anything, "Oh, you're going to Ohio?"

He stared at me incredulously, and I wondered why in the world I had said it. Except that I knew and it was natural to say it. Nothing

153

like that had ever happened to me before. It didn't seem to be anything profound. I simply knew. The way I know my name is Betty Swinford.

Finally, the man stammered, "Wh-why yes. We're going to Kentucky to see some relatives, then on to Ohio."

He didn't ask me how I had known and I certainly offered no explanation. I knew what God was doing. He was teaching me, showing me how it worked, training me to be sensitive to His Spirit. It was kindergarten material, but He was answering prayer and teaching me.

After a time, we had a new pastor. The power of God was with this man and he moved deeply in the Spirit. Positive that he would understand, I went to him and asked him some of my unanswerable questions. I spoke to him about this remarkable gift and tried to explain that whenever God showed me something, it always proved out. He turned on his heel and walked away from me. I got the old message on the gift of 'suspicion' from the pulpit.

I almost turned my back on this gift. The Lord would reveal situations that could have been prevented from happening if someone would have listened to me and guided me. But no one can rise higher than their leader, and certainly no one can take authority over them. And so, the Lord kept teaching me patiently on the ways of the Spirit and showing me that when He spoke, that's just the way it was going to be. The real 'knowing' was still there, whether I could talk to anyone about it or not.

A young woman who was from the Pilgrim Holiness church (now Wesleyan) came into our midst hungry for the infilling of the Spirit. Diligently she sought God for months. Seemingly, she could not receive the baptism in the Spirit. The Lord showed two of us, me and a Southern Baptist friend what the difficulties were. Our friend was seized upon by doubts, fears and unbelief.

One night at the altar we went to prayer with her and gently confronted her with these problems. She confessed them, weeping. Two nights later she was filled with the Spirit.

So, the word of knowledge is not the gift of "suspicion". It is pure, flowing, clear-cut and final. It is literally Thus saith the Lord' and should be allowed to operate through pure persons in the same manner as any other gift. It is always accurate, and it will cleanse, heal and transform.

But let's take a further look at what the gift of the word of knowledge is not. It is not a spirit of divination, Satan's counterfeit. Paul came to the Corinthians by wisdom and revelation. Revelation is insight, knowing. Sometimes it's a mental picture of a situation, yet not a vision. Paul perceived when a certain man had faith to be healed. *Acts 14:8, 9* Paul knew the power and the value of this much treasured gift and he held it very highly. When he used it, something happened. He knew the Spirit who *"searches all things, yea, the deep things of God" (I Cor. 2:10)*.

My pastor once asked me to pay a visit to a Methodist woman who had begun attending services at our church. (You see, the charismatic move at its beginning struck our church full blast, and we enjoyed the flow of the Spirit, the freshness of the denominations and all the dynamics of God's new move in the last days.) This lady was evidently hungry for spiritual reality.

I paid her a visit and all that my pastor had told me seemed to be true. She was excited, eager and appeared to be teachable at that point.

However, before she received a sure knowledge of the Lord Jesus Christ, she attended a meeting where a man with a dubious ministry laid hands on her. It was generally known that this man was possessed of a spirit of divination. The Methodist woman was hungry for something in spiritual experience and she received something. She received a like spirit, a spirit of divination.

The anointing of God comes upon an individual through the laying on of hands. It is transmitted, not the Spirit, but the anointing. The anointing, then, acts as a highway or a conduit through which the Spirit comes.

A pseudo anointing can also be transmitted through the laying on of hands. And whatever spirit is in that false anointing can enter a life. Remember Paul's warning to Timothy about the wrong laying on of hands.

You say, "But what about the eleventh chapter of Luke? Doesn't it say that I f a person asks for the Holy Spirit, he cannot get anything but the Holy Spirit?"

This is indeed true. But the question of her salvation was never settled. Had she been a blood-bought Christian who was asking for the Holy Spirit, it would have been a different matter. But this woman had attended for long years a church where salvation was not preached. She wanted an experience, a feeling.

The counterfeit spirit began to function at once. Awakened at 3:30 a.m. Fran said Jesus was standing at her bedside. Such living fear seized her that she hid under the covers. Later, chilling violently, she peeked again. He was still there. Her body grew so rigid and cold with fear that her husband reported later he could feel the cold in her body without touching her.

The following day a male voice spoke to her from the bedroom. It told her to go to the Holy Land and be baptized in the River

Jordan. Brochures began coming through the mail scheduling tours for the Holy Land.

My pastor became alarmed and asked me to pay her another visit. Something was very wrong with her spiritual experience. I went.

Viewed one way, my visit to her home was a pilgrimage through a valley of fearsome giants. Viewed another, it was a post graduate course in the school of the Spirit, the greatest university in the world.

Fran was ecstatic. She 'knew things' before they happened. She saw bright lights on the mountains, felt the (a) spirit in the dusty whirlwinds that swept her desert home. 'The mailman is just around the corner," she said. "Oh, you can't see him yet! But I know he's there, and in just a minute going to stop at my box and leave another brochure on the Holy Land.'

He did. That's exactly how it happened. She knew all sorts of things before they actually transpired.

Then it came. The crucial test. She asked me to go to her bedroom to pray with her before I left. (Her children in the other parts of the house would have been a hindrance.) I wasn't particularly fond of the idea but consented anyway. After all, I'd prayed with a lot of friends in a lot of bedrooms, so I didn't think too much about it. Until she locked the door, that is. I decided, as the teenagers say, to play it cool.

I knelt on one side of the bed, she on the other. But almost instantly a strange and alien presence drifted into that room. Clearly it was an angel of light. A spirit of divination, a religious spirit, a fortune-telling spirit, spirit of deception — they're really all first cousins. I felt them and I didn't like what I felt. I wanted out!

And suddenly she reached across the bed and grabbed my wrists. "It's coming!" she cried eagerly. "Betty, it's coming!"

I didn't know what was coming and I don't have a spirit of fear, but I wanted to get out of there!

Fran began to 'prophesy'. I was to go with her to the Holy Land. We would be on TV together. Since she couldn't speak, I would be her handmaiden, her spokeswoman. We would stand on top of Mount Moriah, the two of us, before a great stone altar with horns at either end and black snakes crawling all over the ground at our feet. We would be wearing floor length robes of white, fine linen with bells and pomegranates around the hems.

At the foot of the mountain three figures would emerge, Moses, David and Elijah, dressed in sheep skins.

I was praying silently and desperately for wisdom. This thing was just too absurd, and even a kindergarten pupil like me knew it!

But every good liar throws in an element of truth. This throws a person off guard and gives him a greater tendency to believe the whole thing. Here's what she said:

"You have a son, Betty," she said suddenly. "He's twelve years old and has red hair and freckles. Through the years he has given you much sorrow and trouble, and once your nerves broke as a result of the trouble."

I was totally unprepared for this, and remember I was still new in the Spirit. Only recently had I been baptized in the Spirit, having come out of a denominational church where the truth of the Spirit's filling was not preached. Could a wrong spirit really give out all this information?

She proceeded to relate to me some things that happened the days when my nerves had begun to crash. She said, "Your son is not living with you now but with relatives."

"With my sister," I said wonderingly, still in abject unbelief over the other things she had seen. "His eyes are as blue as the sapphire on your finger. No, they're not! They're yellowish-green like a wild coyote's." She meditated silently for a moment. "In three days, you will receive a letter from your sister, and in the letter, she will say, 'He looked at me and he was well.' "

I knew the cunning trick Satan was trying to play on me. He was throwing out an element of truth to try and make me buy the whole package. As soon as it was convenient, I got out of that locked bedroom and went home.

Three days later a letter came from sister. She said, "Get your son out of our house. We're all on tranquillizers and we can't take any more." The devil had overplayed his hand.

A divining spirit is always a little particle of truth mixed with a whole lot of error.

No, the precious gift of the word of knowledge is not a spirit of divination. You can readily see how a spirit of divination and a religious spirit walk hand in hand. Paul was followed by days, remember, by a certain damsel? She was telling the truth about Paul being a man of God, and she was very religious about it. But she was also a diviner or fortune-teller, and her masters made great gain of her.

Fran passed out of my life as she had come into it, quietly and quickly. She was unteachable and she was not looking for help.

It is not some sixth sense. An evangelist from the Christian and Missionary Alliance denomination moves very beautifully in this gift. We shall call him Rev. Blake.

Rev. Blake was holding a revival in the C. & M. A. church once. Traveling with him was a young minister whom we shall call Earl. Rev. Blake was training Earl in the ministry in much the same way as a doctor would train an intern.

One afternoon as Rev. Blake was relaxing in their bedroom at a motel, Earl was in the kitchen writing to his. girlfriend. In order to make an impression on her, he exaggerated on some particular happening in the meeting. Suddenly a voice boomed out of the bedroom.

"Earl, you'd better erase what you just told Kathy. Because it (whatever it was) didn't happen the way you're telling it."

That wasn't E.S.P., sixth sense or mere jesting. That was the word of knowledge, pure and simple, and it nearly startled Earl right out of his skin.

The gift of the word of knowledge is not mind reading, although once in a great while it may happen like that. After all, Jesus knew their thoughts. He knew what was in man.

Once in a meeting in Nebraska the Lord showed me what a prominent lady in the church had said about me. I called it out in the service, told nearly verbatim what she had said but did not let the people know who the woman was. I also told the people that this individual had told these things to a sixteen-year-old boy. You never saw a woman so uncomfortable through an entire service as she was. Later she came to me, confessed the whole thing and apologized. The matter put a godly fear into her.

Neither is it 'soul power', something conjured up from the inner part of the individual. Watchman Nee's book on "The Latent Power of the Soul" deals with this very thing. Soul power, or any power of knowledge brought to the surface from the soulish area of man (remember that can be ego, pride, the will to choose and even the ability to exploit.) In the soul lies the affections and desires, the part of us that Satan touches so often, or dangles temptation before. For he knows all too well the power of the soul. He used his sway over Eve in the very beginning, starting with the body, then causing her to choose.

Choice comes from the soulish part of us. If any individual should attempt to conjure up some sort of knowledge from the soulish area, that knowledge would bring depression. A kind of dark shadow would begin to hang over the life. No profit would be gained. But the true word of knowledge always brings joy, peace and a deep wonderful release. It brings healings in a dozen different ways. No, the word of knowledge never is conjured up from the soul but is divinely implanted into our spirit by a sovereign God.

Again, it is the Holy Spirit searching out all things, yes, the deep things Of God. For God has never lost His power or His knowledge; it is still available and very workable. It is ours to walk with Him day by day and to trust His leadership completely; for the One who redeemed us will never tell us wrong, never lead us astray. His Spirit is a Spirit of truth.

The word of knowledge is not fakery. It is not something 'thought up' to toss out to a congregation at random.

Once I held a revival meeting in a certain state, and, though the meeting took place in an Assembly of God church, it turned out to be a Nazarene revival. Old and young came to the meeting night after night, filling the church. Every age person was slain by the power of God and many of them received the infilling of the Holy Spirit and spoke with tongues.

One of these Nazarenes later went to visit her parents in another state, and while there attended a large charismatic meeting. The speaker continually called out things, then told people they were healed.

My friend called me on the phone to relate the happenings in the meeting. It was wonderful, she said, how he would tell

161

someone, for instance, that they had cancer. The person would not know he had cancer. The evangelist would pray for him, declare that he had been healed of a cancer that he had not even known existed and the speaker said miracles were happening constantly.

There was something about this that bothered me. I asked my Nazarene friend if these illnesses were confirmed.

"Oh no," she said. "He just tells people what's wrong with them and then prays and they're healed."

"How do they know they're healed if they didn't know they were sick?" I asked.

There was a moment of silence. "I never really thought about that." She hesitated. "He just said that the people were healed and miracles were taking place and everyone seemed to believe him."

I had not meant to plant doubts in her mind, but it was necessary that she begin to see that much of what is acclaimed today as being the word of knowledge in operation is nothing more than self-exploitation. And it is so easy to get into a new relationship with God and it's all so thrilling and so much is happening that is genuine and wonderful that persons can become very gullible without even knowing it.

Unless the word of knowledge is confirmed. it is of little or no value. The Holy Spirit begins immediately to minister to the person whose ailment has been called out, the word is confirmed, a healing takes place and the individual will either at that time or a later time testify to that healing.

I suppose anyone could stand before a congregation and call out a stomach ulcer, even tell a specific person that he or she had a stomach ulcer.

The person might say, "But I've never been told that I have an ulcer."

And if the one ministering is suffering from self-esteem or if he is coveting this beautiful gift and is copying it badly, he may say, "Well, but you do have an ulcer. Now I'm going to pray for you and you'll be healed." So, he prays and declares that the healing has taken place, when all the time the person in question never knew anything about the ulcer, its position in the stomach or its healing.

It just does not work that way. The word of knowledge is clear and the person identifies easily when the word is spoken. That word becomes alive within them and they know God is speaking about them. They reach out in new faith and the healing is completed. And, believe me, it can bear the mark of a doctor's exam years afterward.

Day before yesterday a letter came in the mail from a woman in Boulder, Colorado who was healed of a hernia by the operation of the gift of the word of knowledge nearly three years ago. She said she had had to go to a doctor to be X-rayed for some new condition in her body and there was absolutely no sign of the old hernia.

It may be well to remember that there must be a real before there can be a counterfeit. In fact, there can be no counterfeit unless there is the real. After all, who would counterfeit one-hundred-dollar bills if there were no hundred-dollar bills?

We are admonished to *"Prove all things; hold fast that which is good" (I Thess. 5:21).* No matter what Little Miss Muffet or Mr. Jack Horner or even an angel from heaven comes to you with 'a word from the Lord', toss it into the garbage can if it cannot be squared with the Word of God. Even if it can, shelve it. If God is saying something to you, He will bring it all to pass in due time.

163

No glory must ever be given to any individual who is used by the Holy Spirit in this wonderful gift. Esteem it highly. Let it flow through your life to others. But it must be manifested skillfully and with wisdom, for great responsibility goes with the gifts of God. And never, never let it be used for any kind of personal exploit.

Chapter Four

OLD TESTAMENT SEERS

The gift of the word of knowledge is not something new that was given to believers with the outpouring of the Holy Spirit in the Book of Acts. To the contrary, the word of knowledge has been manifested by the Spirit all through the word of God, and the Old Testament gives us some outstanding examples of the ways this gift operated away back there.

Men who walked deeply with God and spent time lingering in His presence were also men who were mightily used of God. Not all of them were used in the operation of this gift, as not every believer is used in this particular gift today. But there were definitely those in Old Testament history upon whom the Spirit would come, and, with His coming, there would be given supernatural knowledge.

Such men were called 'seers', and a seer was simply someone who 'saw into'.

The prophet Elisha is a beautiful example of a man of God through whom the Spirit manifested this flowing gift. It might do well, however, to remember that Elisha was a man who thirsted after God. And he didn't give up until he caught the mantle of the fiery prophet Elijah as it floated back down out of the skies. Elisha was from that time forth a mighty Spirit-filled, Spirit-led man who knew how to respond to the Lord and be used of Him. All too often today we see those whose dedications are questionable, yet who desire and even try within themselves to be used in this beautiful, healing gift of the word of knowledge.

Elisha was up on Mt. Carmel. He hadn't the remotest idea that anything was wrong in the home where he was living. He saw the Shunammite woman coming in the distance and sent his servant — who was not too trusty an individual as we shall soon see — to inquire about her and her family. Although the report came back that all was well when the woman reached the prophet, she fell to the ground at his feet in anguish. If he could have been used in the word of knowledge at that point, he would have unlocked the silent agony of her soul. But the knowledge simply was not there, and he made this statement: *"The Lord hath hidden it from me and hath not told me."*

This gift of supernatural, God-given knowledge may flow through an individual for weeks, and suddenly you don't know anything. It is as though you were never used in this particular manner at all. If God doesn't show a person, he simply doesn't know. Not even the godly prophet Elisha. He was as blank as a wall without pictures. And he never did know what the problem was until she told him.

Yet in other instances Elisha saw perfectly, both by knowledge and by revelation. (Sometimes knowledge and revelation are so closely related as to be unable to separate them.)

When the king of Syria declared war against Israel, he instructed his servants to make camp for him "in such and such a place." Elisha knew the plans and the words spoken by the king of Syria and immediately squelched those plans by making them known to the king of Israel. And because of the word of knowledge working in Elisha's life, the king was spared. According to *II Kings 6:10*, he was saved several times.

166

Can't you just imagine the Syrian king's chagrin when he cried out, "But how did Elisha know? I made those plans in my own bedroom!"

But the story goes on. The king of Syria is out to get even. He sends a host of horses and chariots and surrounds the city of Dothan where Elisha was at that time. There they were, lying in wait, when Elisha's servant went outside and saw the Syrian army. He came immediately to warn the prophet.

Elisha went to take a look and turned to his servant quickly to speak words of reassurance. Now the spirit of revelation was functioning through the prophet's life, and he was seeing with the eyes of his spirit what his natural eyes could never have beheld. He said, in effect, "Don't worry. There's an army out there to fight for us that far outnumbers the men in the Syrian army. "

Then he prayed, and his prayer was that the Lord would open the young servant's eyes to see what Elisha saw. And through the eyes of the Spirit, it was revealed to the men that God had sent His heavenly army to defend the prophet. For they saw that the mountains were filled with heaven's armies!

Throughout this entire episode both the word of knowledge and revelation were working and flowing beautifully together.

The most outstanding incident in Elisha's life where the Holy Spirit used him in supernatural knowledge was in the case of Naaman the leper.

One cannot place a price tag on any ministry if it is truly born of the Holy Spirit. It would not only be degrading but dishonoring to God. A true ministry will speak for itself, be led supernaturally of the Lord, and gimmicks, bargaining or love for personal gain will have no part in it.

Elisha knew this. But his servant Gehazi did not.

Naaman's healing from leprosy was a simple cure once he was willing to take it. Leaving the muddy waters of the Jordan River with his disease gone and his flesh cleansed, Naaman went back and stood before Elisha. Now he wanted to pay him for the miracle.

Now, let's don't get side-tracked or get any mistaken ideas here. They who preach the Gospel must also live by it, and the laborer is worthy of his hire. But Naaman was not learned in spiritual things enough to know the difference. He was not desiring to support Elisha's ministry; he wanted to pay for his miracle. And that's where Elisha was wise. For the miracle did not come from him but from the God of miracles. You just can't put a price tag on a miracle that God, through His sovereign grace and mercy, performs.

Elisha refused any remuneration, even though Naaman urged him to receive a gift. And Elisha sent him on his way in peace.

But Gehazi had other ideas. Paraphrasing Swinford-style, the servant said to himself; "It's one thing for Elisha to turn down a gift, but I'm out to get what I can!" Gehazi ran after Naaman's chariot and met with him face to face.

"Is everything all right?" Naaman asked.

"Everything's great," Gehazi assured the Syrian. "But there are a couple of Bible school students from Mount Ephriam who have come to visit me and Elisha would appreciate it if you would give them some silver and two new suits of clothes."

"Oh, let me do better than that," Naaman urged. "I'll give you twice as much silver that you asked for in two bags and two changes of clothing too."

And that scoundrel took his loot and hid it in his house and then went to stand before Elisha. Whether Elisha sent for him we don't know. "Where've you been?" Elisha asked casually.

"Who me?" Gehazi shrugged. "Why, I haven't been anywhere."

And Elisha looked him straight in the eye and said, "Ah, Gehazi, you didn't know it but I knew exactly what you've been doing every moment. None of your activity has been hidden from me. I know it all."

And Gehazi froze before the man of God. When the Holy Spirit chooses to reveal, nothing can escape that searching gaze. Gehazi's sin had been known by Elisha all the time, and that servant went from the presence of the prophet a leper as white as snow. Naaman's past illness was fastened upon Gehazi for the rest of his life.

This is an outstanding and perfect manifestation of the operation of the gift of the word of knowledge.

When God reveals a thing, it is crystal clear. When He chooses to hide something from us, we cannot see it no matter how hard we may try.

Many times, in the Old Testament days individuals would come into a strange town and seek out a seer for direction in some given matter. These seers were not fortune tellers. They were men who walked with God in deep fellowship and paid frequent visits to their own personal Holy of Holies where they lingered in that divine Presence. There, they learned to know His ways and His voice. Then, when someone came to them for direction or a word from the Lord, the knowledge that came forth was clean, pure and authentic.

Kathryn Kuhlman said of the Holy Spirit that He is "a most colorful personality", and He most surely is. Not just a feeling or an influence but as much of a Person as the Father and the Son.

He is a Person who feels, understands and has perfect knowledge. He can be grieved, resisted and quenched.

Symbolically, He is as gentle as a dove, as powerful as an earthquake or as fierce as a flame of fire. He is also loving and comforting; yet He is as piercing as a dart and knows all the thoughts and intents of the heart. He is as paradoxical as the other members of the Trinity.

The Holy Spirit has a very fine sense of humor. This is so beautifully illustrated in the story of King Jeroboam's wife.

The king had a son named Abijah who became ill. Jeroboam said to his wife, "I want you to put on a disguise so you won't be known as my wife. Take ten loaves of bread, some cakes and a cruise of honey and go to Shiloh. There's a prophet there by the name of Ahijah who told me that I would be king.

"You give him this food and he'll tell you what's going to happen to our son."

So, Jeroboam's wife put on a disguise. The Bible doesn't tell us what sort of disguise it was, but certainly it was one that did not speak of queenliness. Maybe she went dressed as a peasant woman. We can only speculate. At any rate, she obeyed her husband and went to Shiloh. Apparently, she didn't know that the prophet Ahijah was blind and wouldn't have recognized her anyway.

But God was not silent. He was speaking to Ahijah and telling him that Jeroboam's wife was coming to ask about her son, because he was sick. And by the time the wife of the king drew near and Ahijah could hear the sound of her footsteps, the Lord had told him the whole plot. She would come pretending to be another woman. Then God instructed Ahijah as to what he should say to her.

She got to the door, perfectly assured that her disguise was perfect and she would fool this man of God completely. He would never guess who she really was.

Can you see her fallen countenance, her collapsed composure, her absolute unbelief when she heard the startling words: "Come in, thou wife of Jeroboam. "

He spoke so calmly as to shake her to the very depths. Then he asked her the question, "What do you think you're doing, anyway, pretending to be some other woman?"

Surely, he must have been chuckling inside. And surely the Holy Spirit was smiling, too, at this humorous scene.

There are many other instances in the Old Testament where the word of knowledge was used through various individuals. Supernatural knowledge was manifested in the life of Isaiah. The story can be found in the book of *Isaiah, chapter 7, verses 3* and *4.*

It was poured through Joshua after the defeat of Israel at Ai. First God showed Joshua that there was sin in the camp. Next the man Achan was called out. Joshua said to him, "Tell me now what thou hast done; hide it not from me." And Achan melted before that God-given knowledge and confessed his theft of the gold, silver and beautiful Babylonian garments. The result was death, to him and to all that belonged to him, both family and animals.

In *II Samuel 24:11* we read of a man named Gad, who was 'David's seer'. And in *I Samuel 9:9* these words are penned; *"Previously in Israel, when a man went to inquire of God, thus he spoke, 'Come, and let us go to the seer'; for he that is now called a prophet was formerly called a seer."*

The late A. W. Tozer says that the mind should be an eye to see with and a bin to store facts in. He declares that the man who has been taught and schooled by the Spirit will be a seer instead of a scholar. And there is a major difference between the two. For the scholar sees, but the seer sees into.

Chapter Five

A SPIRIT OF REVELATION

Just what does that word 'revelation' mean, anyway? Well, Webster says it means an 'act of revealing'. It's also God's revelation to man and also the last book in the Bible. Another dictionary says that revelation means an 'act of revealing', 'something revealed' or 'an enlightening or astonishing disclosure'.

That's really it. A revelation is an enlightening or — and sometimes and — an astonishing disclosure.

Paul desired that we have a spirit of revelation and our hearts be flooded with light. And when our hearts are flooded with light like a flash of lightning the Holy Spirit discloses something to us! and that is a spirit of revelation.

Sometimes it may be a swift quickening of the Word. It appears that certain verses have leaped up from the page, so alive to your heart does the Word become. You embrace it, taste its sweetness, glory in its truth. You have had a revelation of the Word and your heart has been filled and flooded with heaven's light. There's a lot of beauty and dignity in that.

Other times, swiftly as a soaring eagle, God shows you a truth in the inner man. With this truth there may come a picture — not a vision — but a mental picture. That too is a revelation. Let me illustrate.

One time just after the tremendous outpouring of the Spirit of God swept my city, a great nucleus of Methodist folk was gathered into this wondrous outpouring. On fire for God, yet never having been schooled or trained in spiritual things. some of them began to go off on little side trips. (Fortunately, nearly all of them came back to basic truth and are in sound evangelical churches today.)

During this period of time my path crossed with Shelly Martin. It crossed, as a matter of fact, on the telephone. She was going through an extreme trial and would like to talk with me. I agreed to come to her home since she didn't have a car at hand.

On a Tuesday noon I drove through the city to Shelly's home. We spent time talking and praying and she began to open her heart to me.

It seems that she had gone to a denominational church where she had heard there were some Spirit-filled believers. After the preaching she went to the altar to pray, and while she was praying, she broke out praying in tongues.

But to her utter chagrin, everyone else who was praying near her at the altar rose hastily to their feet and started to the door. The minister's treatment of this beautiful Christian was much the same as he would have given someone with the black plague.

Wounded in her spirit and the Spirit Himself grieved within her, she lay and wept for days. What had she done wrong? Would she do it again? Weren't other Spirit-filled people as free in their spirits as she felt in hers? These and a hundred other questions pounded at her weary brain, until she reached a point where, red-faced and swollen-eyed, she could think no more.

It's really wonderful to see how people are healed when they confess and get their burdens out into the open. The enemy has no more power to hurt and torment once an individual has 'cleared the deck', so to speak, in their own hearts.

Shelly spoke much of two close friends from the same denomination. One was a man who had helped her much, she

174

said, after being filled with the Spirit. The other was a woman, rather strange but still a good friend. I listened quietly and thought little about her two much-alluded-to friends. Until we were eating lunch.

The doorbell rang and Shelly went to answer it. There stood a tall, rather good-looking man who kissed her lightly and came into the room. He stopped short, however, when he saw me, and his expression changed as though a mask had been slipped from his face.

"Oh — ! I didn't know you had company."

My new friend was fairly dancing around the room. She was like a lovely golden elf who was free to flit and dance and be free. "Oh, Keith, this is Betty Swinford. Betty, this is my very dear friend Keith Elmore. He's been my spiritual guide and counselor since being filled with the Holy Spirit. We've had such a beautiful relationship.

I greeted him, but inwardly I felt deeply troubled. I kept telling myself how ridiculous it was to feel this way when I had just met the man. I wasn't being fair to him! Nevertheless, something was wrong about their relationship. Not on her part, perhaps, but on his.

We were served cake and sat around the table sharing Christ, when suddenly Keith put his fork down and bowed his head. Evidently this was some sort of signal, because Shelly immediately copied him. And not wanting to resist or grieve the Spirit if He was wanting to do something, I likewise bowed my head. He waited.

Soon Keith began softly mumbling his way through a strange prayer. It sounded more like a chant or incantation than it did a prayer, really. Another deep pause, while an alien spirit floated into the room with us.

I thought, "Oh God, that's the same spirit I felt in that locked bedroom with Fran! Lord, please show me whatever it is you're trying to make clear to me."

Then Keith began quoting scripture from the books of Isaiah and Joel. And he was acting as though he were prophesying to Shelly by his quotes. His voice was low, almost crooning. The presence of this other spirit clearly as an angel of light grew stronger and stronger. Then Keith gave direct quotes from Isaiah to my new friend quotes that could never in any way be meant for any one person or any group of people on the face of the earth except the Jews and their return to Palestine.

When the time was fairly appropriate, I excused myself and started for home. I was sick in the pit of my stomach.

While driving up through the foothills to my home, suddenly, with no forethought of any kind, there bolted before my vision a clear, keen picture. It was not a vision. I've never had a vision. It was a revelation, a strong mental picture that fairly swept before me. I saw Shelly, and I saw two other persons standing, one on either side of her. One was a white-haired woman, an elderly woman. The other was Keith Elmore. Together, they were literally pressing the life out of my friend! It was also very evident that Keith was in love with Shelly, and, even though she was a wife and the mother of four teenage daughters, he meant to have her. (He was also married.)

I said, "Oh dear Lord, what shall I do? I can't tell anyone, it's far too personal to share. Yet You've shown me this thing for some reason." I was breathless and stunned over what I had seen and was still seeing. Then the Lord showed me that the elderly woman was in witchcraft and was literally calling up spirits from the dead. (Or at least familiar spirits, those spirits who can take on the voice and appearance of those who have died.) The Holy Spirit had never shown me anything like that before, never spoken to me or imparted knowledge in exactly this way. The Lord's presence in the car was exceedingly precious, so different from the counterfeit spirit I had just left behind me.

"Father, what shall I do with this information?"

He said clearly, "Nothing. Wait until I tell you to speak."

Now I am aware of the fact that a lot of Christians don't think that God still speaks to His children today, and I'm sorry because that point of view is just not scriptural. The problem is not with God speaking. The problem is that His children are not listening. If we learn to wait in His presence, He has something to say to us.

Three months passed by. The bruising on this delicate woman's spirit over her experience at the denominational altar didn't heal overnight. But gradually, as she continually yielded herself to the master Physician, He who came to heal the broken hearted and to set at liberty them that are bruised, set the healing processes flowing in her spirit.

One night I was prompted to call Shelly and tell her what I had seen that afternoon after leaving her home. I couldn't bring myself to do it. The prompting came again. I said, "Lord, she's been through so much. How can I tell her what I saw in the Spirit and hurt her again? Besides, she loves those two people. She probably wouldn't even believe this came from You."

The Lord impressed me for the third time to pick up the telephone and call her. I sighed and looked at the clock. It was after nine o'clock, so it was probably too late any- -

The phone rang beside me. I picked it up and heard Shelly's voice on the line. "Betty, I really don't know why I'm calling you. I just felt so impressed that I should do it, so — here I am."

From that point I proceeded as gently as possible to relate to her the revelation the Lord had given. And, as I spoke, it became the word of knowledge.

She didn't resist the things God had shown me, though at the time I confess that I wasn't too sure. Later, however, I discovered that the man in question did make it clear to her that he had designs on her and the relationship was immediately dissolved. (Just prior to this the two people had come to see her together. After they left Shelly fell into a strange illness that left her considerably weakened, to the point where her life hung in the balance.)

A very short time elapsed when we found that the elderly woman was indeed calling up spirits and holding seances.

Today Shelly is a vibrant Christian and God alone is her stabilizer.

Many of the ancients (whose writings are scarcely read in our day of instant television saints and converted playboys) had revelations of God, and by the eye of faith entered into the sweet mysteries of God and the realities of our Lord Jesus Christ.

St. Augustine, for example, had such a revelation of Jesus that he was compelled to pen these words, "1 came to love You late, O Beauty so ancient and new; I came to love You late. You were within me and I was outside, where I rushed about wildly, searching for You like some monster loose in Your beautiful world. You were with me, but I was not with You. You called to me. You shouted to me. You broke past my deafness: You bathed with your life: You wrapped me in Your splendor: You sent my blindness reeling. You gave out such a delightful fragrance and I drew it in and came breathing hard after you. I tasted it and it made me hunger and thirst: You touched me and I burned to know your Presence."

And a man by the name of Ramon Lull, a Catholic lay preacher in the 1200's had such a knowledge and revelation of the Saviour that he wrote of the Lover (himself) and the Saviour (the Beloved) meeting one another one day, He said the Beloved reached out to embrace the Lover, He leaned down to kiss him, but He remained ever on high that the Lover might ever seek Him.

There is a revelation of truth!

Richard Rolle spoke of knowing the Lord so intimately that He would become to us heat and fragrance and song. Gerhard Tersteegen speaks softly of the hidden love of God.

These and a grand, unnumbered host of others had such revelations of God and His ways and His word that changed their lives and kept them from the dreary hum-drum of life that has become the way for many Christians.

A true revelation does what it is supposed to do. It reveals. Haven't you heard someone say, ¡ 'Why, I've read that scripture a thousand times, and all of a sudden it leaped at me from the pages! I really saw and understood it!"

A close Lutheran friend had a revelation of what it means to pray in the spirit. She was praying •very earnestly in tongues one day when she saw herself standing in a kind of courtyard. God was sitting upon His throne (she didn't see His face) and Christ was sitting on His right hand. As she prayed, she saw tens of thousands of angels bow to the ground on either side of her and fold their wings in awe and respect. Her Great High Priest stood and leaned forward to listen intently to the language she was speaking.

Her sub-conscious was astonished that He would take such notice of her prayer, that she was commanding the attention of all heaven. And then the Lord showed her that heaven was not listening to my friend pray, it was listening to the Holy Spirit praying through her. And what He was praying commanded the attention of the angels, of the Father and the Son. And Jesus, who Himself ever lives to make intercession for us, turned and prayed that prayer to the Father.

That was a revelation of prayer in the spirit and it changed her prayer life. We have to conclude, therefore, that a spirit of revelation may be a mental picture with the word of knowledge, or it can be a sudden revealing without the word of knowledge. At any rate, the two are closely related and it would take a very fine line indeed to separate them.

However, an individual may experience a revelation, it is still knowledge received by faith, not by 'sense knowledge' or 'intellectual knowledge' that has been gathered through facts furnished a person by observation.

And, as revelation lies within the horizon of the word of knowledge, so does the word of knowledge fall into the scope of revelation. Any and all knowledge that comes from the Holy Spirit causes one to see by the eye of faith, not with a brain filled with obtained data.

Chapter Six

A HEALING FORCE

*T*he Spirit of the Lord is upon me, because he hath anointed me to preach the gospel to the poor; he hath sent me to heal the broken-hearted, to preach deliverance to the captives, and recovering of sight to the blind, to set at liberty them that are bruised (Luke 4:18).

Although my family came to Christ in the First Baptist Church in West Terre Haute, Indiana, we spent 14 years in the Christian and Missionary Alliance Church in Tucson, Arizona. There are very tender places in our hearts for both of these denominations, for both of them taught us the Word and the value of walking a separated life in God.

In the Missionary Alliance movement, we discovered divine healing, and just at the time when I was suffering intensely with a stomach ulcer. That was the first time healing touched my body and I was healed in a split second, when doctors had not been able to help me during an eight week's stay in the hospital.

Since that time our family has experienced many wonderful healings. Sometimes the healings have come as a result of being anointed with oil, as was the case when our small daughter was healed instantly and miraculously of cancer of the brain. We've been healed through the spoken word, the laying on of hands and simply as the Lord moved upon us sovereignly. Our children have been healed when we have laid hands upon them, and we have been healed when our children have ministered to us.

I used to wonder about the passage of scripture in *I Corinthians 12:9* when Paul speaks about 'the gifts of healing', indicating strongly that there was more than a single gift in divine or spiritual healings.

One person has a gift of imparting healing through the laying on of hands. Another may command healing for an individual. Another may be used in such a manner that, as he is preaching the Word, individuals are healed in his congregation. Yet another may pray with such complete faith that others experience healing.

God has a thousand ways to do it. That's just elementary. He'll out-scheme you every time. You plan a way for God to heal you and He'll come and do it in a way you never heard of or thought about.

Now we know God heals. And we know that He still heals today. So, the subject matter in this particular chapter is not to convince the reader of the healing power of God. Nor is it to elaborate on some of the various methods He uses to heal. Rather, we shall deal in depth with healing as it inter-relates to the word of knowledge.

Even here the inner working of the word of knowledge and healing are very beautiful, yet most varied. For instance, while in a meeting in northern Colorado a beautiful young teenager walked into the morning service. Her life opened to me at a glance. Later she came down the aisle to meet the Lord.

The words prompted by the Holy Spirit were, "You have gone through some great trials for one so young. But there is a sincere hunger in your heart for God. In fact, you have walked with the Lord in the past and then shut Him out of your life." A moment's

182

hesitation. The Holy Spirit was speaking to her and she was deeply moved. "Your father is a minister, isn't he?"

She lifted her head and stared. "Why, yes. How did you know?"

"The Lord showed me. He isn't ministering now, though. He's away somewhere, away from God and — away from you and your mother. Why, this is why you stopped walking with God!"

She laid her head on my shoulder there in that prayer line and wept. We prayed for a healing of her emotions and memories, healing for her broken heart. She received the inner healings and has gone on to Bible College in Texas to study for some type of ministry.

You see, for nearly all of my Christian life — after discovering that God still heals today — I thought He came to heal stomach ulcers, cancer, heart attacks and bad backs. And more. But the Word declares that He came, anointed of God, to heal the brokenhearted, the bruised, the captives.

Oh, there are so many bruised souls today, so many crushed spirits, so many captives! Bruisings and brokenness that have taken place perhaps in childhood. And those bruisings torment with memory, heartbreak and failures. These need healings to take place in the mind, the memory, the emotions, these things that Jesus came to heal.

You say, "But I thought He came to heal arthritis and stomach ulcers."

And what causes stomach ulcers, arthritis and a host of other ailments and diseases? Bitterness, fear, anxiety, heartbreak, bruisings. Poisons are literally introduced into the bloodstream of a person with a bitter spirit, and the result can be – this is not always so! — rheumatoid arthritis.

Jesus came to set the captives free. I have met actually hundreds of Christians, even Spirit-filled Christians, whose lives are eaten up with fear. There is more fear running rampant in our meetings than any other spirit, and, for the person who entertains this enemy, he will soon find himself a miserable captive to the fear syndrome.

Twelfth century Catholic lay minister Ramon Lull said that the more we love God, the more He will attend to our needs. This is truth!

A young Catholic girl came into a service in Missouri one night. The meetings were being held in a denominational church, but the majority of people attending were either Methodists or Catholics. This girl came with several of her Catholic sisters who had already overcome their fears and attended previous meetings.

This teenager sat on the back row, literally shriveled up with fear and insecurity. The Holy Spirit began to illuminate. She was unloved, yet longed with every longing of a young girl's heart to be loved. The impression came very strongly to minister to her. She came into a prayer line at the close of the service and was the last person to be prayed for. I touched her gently and spoke as the Lord had already directed.

"You have a great sense of loneliness within you and a feeling that you are not loved." She began to tremble visibly. "There is a longing in your heart for love. God wants you to know that He loves you, and I want you to know that I love you."

She crumbled, clutched me with both arms and wept on my shoulder. Her life was transformed.

The next day the minister said to me, "Have you heard about Norene?"

"What do you mean?"

"She came to church with two of her sisters last night. Did you know that?"

184

"Yes," I replied wonderingly.

The minister smiled. "But you don't know what she said on the way to church, do you?"

I shrugged. "Why, no. I haven't the vaguest idea."

"She said, 'I would give anything in this world if just one person would say to me, 'I love you.' "

The sheer beauty of it! The tender evidence of God's care. He saw the deep-seated need and came to heal that inner part of Norene that was reaching out for healing. Neglected by her drinking mother, deserted by her father, she was indeed a teenager who needed love. But the lovely miracle was that the God of eternal ages would come to tell her that He loved her.

Yes, the operation of the gift of the word of knowledge is a healing force. God reveals. He speaks. And when He speaks faith rises within the heart and healing is made easy. There is no struggle to receive, for God is saying, 'Here it is. I have it all for you. I'm aware of your need."

Healing as relating to the word of knowledge can come in many ways. God is so great; He never falls in a stereotyped pattern as we sometimes do. Rather He is a God of variety and seems to delight in moving out of our pre-designed molds.

I sat down by the pianist one night after a service in Texas. Instantly I was struck by a sharp pain in my right abdomen. For a moment I was mystified. This was something new to me. Gently, ever so gently, the Holy Spirit suggested that I ask the pianist if she ever had a pain in that area.

When I obeyed the Spirit, Doris looked at me with wide gray eyes. "Do I?" she repeated quickly. "Why, I have that pain through every revival meeting because I have to sit at the piano so long. I'm almost to the point where I dread revivals because of the pain."

185

The Spirit was quickened between us. I can't explain that. It wasn't thunder and lightning or even goosebumps! But if you have experienced that you will understand what I'm talking about.

I did not lay hands on her, anoint her with oil or even pray for her. We knew He had already done the work. As soon as the word was spoken, she was quickened and healed. There was no more pain during that meeting.

In April of 1976 I held another meeting in that same place and she told me that she had never been bothered by that pain again.

Many times God attempts to use one of His children in this manner and, not understanding what it's all about, they think the pain or ailment is their own and so accept it and settle down to try and get rid of it. I was doing this same thing until my pastor, who was watching my ministry develop, said, "Sister, I just don't believe all these things belong to you."

I called him by name, a precious brother in Christ. "I don't know what you mean."

"I mean," he said, "that I think these things you experience are for someone else. If you'll begin to pray about this, the Lord will show you who the sickness or pain is for."

That's just the way it was. Now it has happened to me many hundreds of times, sometimes alone with a friend, sometimes when I am in the pulpit, other times when I am on my way to a meeting. And the very moment I release what I am feeling by calling it out over a congregation and pray for the individual who is troubled by the thing, — whether it be pain, sickness, fear, bitterness, torment or whatever — I am immediately delivered from it and so is the person prayed for.

Other times the individual will have such faith sweep into him that he needs no prayer and no laying on of hands. The word itself

186

does the healing as it is accepted. Remember, "He sent His word and healed them."

A man came into the prayer line in a large charismatic church in a certain city. Dirty, shaggy-haired and unkept, he was probably in his early forties. His eyes were bloodshot and it was all too evident that he was a hopeless alcoholic. And because the Holy Spirit is never repulsed or 'turned off' to man's failures and frailties, compassion swept in. God was looking, not at the man but at the man behind the man. He was looking at all that had caused him to become an alcoholic and all that he could be if delivered.

Hands were laid upon this man and the Lord began to reveal his past failures and feelings of despair. So far as he was concerned, there was no help; but the Lord assured him that, because He saw and understood, He would do something about it.

Such power flowed that this six-foot, some odd inches of bone and muscle fell flat on his back. A short time later, however, he was back for prayer. Could he have the laying on of hands one more time? He knew God had touched him, but he must have more!

The phenomenon that followed was something that none of us had ever witnessed before and have never witnessed again.

The man did not fall under the power. He turned around and started to return to his seat, when he discovered that he was glued to the floor! Literally, he was glued and could not pick up either of his feet. At first, he laughed. Then he cried. Then he prayed. For thirty minutes this giant of a man stood there unable to move. He was nailed to that floor.

When finally he could take steps, it looked as if he were pulling one foot at a time, with great struggle, from thick glue. It was thirty minutes more before he could reach the car, where his father was waiting with joy to take him home.

That was the end of the alcoholic. I saw him a month later and at first glance did not recognize him. Here sat a shining Christian whose face fairly glowed with an inner light. His hair was well groomed, his eyes were clear and direct, and his clothes were clean and well-fitting, He was transformed, aglow with the Spirit of God. He has never been the same man to this day; simply because the Holy Spirit saw beyond the alcoholic into his deep-seated inner need. And when the man discovered that God was concerned about him, and that this concern would meet and fully satisfy his deeper need, hope and faith had leaped upwards and his soul's cry was fully satisfied.

A woman who attended a denominational church in a certain city in Arizona was moved upon by the Spirit to lay hands on a crippled woman who was sitting in the aisle in a wheel chair. My friend we shall call her Helen — immediately began trying to bargain with God. A timid woman by nature, she began to quake inwardly. Oh! How God loves to use the weak, the foolish, the despised!

"Now, Lord," she began silently, "You know how sick Chris Hanson's baby has been. I'll lay hands on the baby. But please get someone else to lay hands on Margaret." After all, Margaret had been confined to a wheel chair for many years. To touch her and command her to walk — !

The Lord said, "Helen, go lay hands on Margaret and tell her to rise and walk in My name."

"God," she said, trembling from head to foot, "I just can't do that. But I'm willing to lay hands on Chris' baby and trust You to heal him."

The impression came again, and it was much too clear to ignore without willfully resisting the Spirit. If Helen would obey, Margaret would walk again.

The Holy Spirit was moving that Sunday morning in such a manner that it was perfectly in order for Helen to take such a step. Various individuals were ministering to one another.

Helen stepped out, and as she did so the Spirit came upon her with great power. Taking the hands of the crippled woman, there was no fear now! — she spoke with authority. "In the name of Jesus, rise and walk!" And Margaret did just that. Beautifully so. She walked straight down the aisle, took the microphone from the pastor and proclaimed her healing.

Now the working of the word of knowledge in this incident is quite different and relatively simple. Nevertheless, as the knowledge was obeyed and the word spoken, the outcome was the same as in the previous incident.

Yes, . . . *"there are diversities of gifts, but the same Spirit. And there are differences of administrations, but the same Lord. And there are diversities of operations, but it is the same God who worketh all in all"* (*I Cor. 12:4-6*).

Various gifts, different administrations and many, many ways to operate His gifts. Yet they are all in control of and flow from the same Holy Spirit who anoints them to bring forth fruit to the glory of God.

It is indeed unfortunate that there are those individuals who feel a need to help the Holy Spirit in governing the gifts, or trying to bring Him to the point of channeling the gifts down some manmade avenue.

See the word of knowledge as a silver dart piercing between facade and reality, soul and spirit, need and desire. See it as pure blazing light that penetrates through and through, going straight to the source of need and, in a moment's time, fully meeting that intricate need.

Then let's see where 'man helps' interrupt that flow of knowledge to probe, search, dig and sometimes destroy. For instance, God is mightily using Christian psychology and psychiatry today in digging problems from individual lives and bringing them to some sort of solution. Some are even exorcising wrong spirits with great success.

However, when God's sovereign knowledge flows from one's life, let's not be mistaken in thinking we need to •add to' what God has already given. For the Holy Spirit can do in a moment what all the sense knowledge of gathered data could take years to accomplish. He alone can transform lastingly, heal memories and emotions and make an individual whole. No frayed ends in God's economy, no struggling to change. He speaks and it is so. He grants a word of knowledge and a life is instantly transformed.

A young woman could not receive from God. One night several people gathered around her at an altar service. Someone forced her arms into the air. Someone else shouted for her to 'let go'. Another person was saying that she was lazy and would not reach for God herself but made others do it for her.

The Holy Spirit was grieved. Compassion began to flow. Words were whispered into her ear, "You may not be able to make an audible sound, but God hears the tears slipping down your face."

Immediately she began to receive from the Lord. God further revealed that deep scars lay upon her memories because of a father who had told her repeatedly during childhood that she was demon possessed. She had lived with this terror all her life. It had dragged at her mind like chains, pulling her down, blocking her spiritual progress and in short — keeping her at a continual low ebb.

Nothing, not psychology or psychiatry, not a high level of knowledge in Greek and Hebrew, can replace the anointing of God upon His own gifts that are given to heal, to bless, to comfort and deliver.

How infinitely great are His workings and His ways past finding out. How He longs with tender longings to meet every need in our lives. Of course, some things do come to bless and heal by natural means. Some things do happen through sense knowledge and circumstance. We don't rule out other methods that God uses to meet us and bring us to Himself. But He is vitally interested in everything that involves the lives of even His lowliest children and will always move to meet their needs and help them.

"He and I in that bright glory,
One great joy we'll share;
Mine, to be forever with Him,
His, that I am there."
--Tersteegen

Chapter Seven

IN THE LIFE OF JESUS

You say, "Oh, now wait a minute! The word of knowledge didn't operate in Jesus' life. He was God and therefore already knew all things."

That is certainly true. He was God, but He was also man. He was God in man, the Word made flesh, majesty and all of heaven's glory dwelling in a temple of clay. As God, He needed no one; as man, He needed someone to stand with Him during the darkest hour of His earthly life. As God, He freely forgives all sin; as man, He understands why sin runs through the human race and how mankind is tested almost beyond endurance. As God, He knew all things; as man, He was totally dependent upon the Holy Spirit, just as you and I are dependent upon Him today.

Before we go any further, let's settle that question. *Acts 10:38* says, *"How God anointed Jesus of Nazareth with the Holy Ghost and with power, who went about doing good and healing all that were oppressed of the devil, for God was with Him."*

Jesus, as man, had to have the same anointing we must have in order to be effective for God. The Spirit of God had to rest upon Him. Jesus was dependent upon the Spirit of God. In *Luke* chapter *4* and *Isaiah chapter 61* we read the words; *"The Spirit of the Lord is upon me, because He hath anointed me — "* Why? To set at

192

liberty them that are bruised, to heal broken hearts, to preach, to loose the captives-

These words are recorded of Jesus in *Luke 5:17, ". . . and the power of the Lord was present for Him to heal them."* Jesus was dependent upon the Holy Spirit in His life and in His death. If the Spirit did not come through after Jesus' death on Calvary, His dying would have been all in vain.

But *Romans 8:11* zeros in with these victorious words, *"But if the Spirit of Him that raised Jesus from the dead dwell in you, He that raised up Christ from the dead shall also quicken your mortal bodies by His Spirit that dwelleth in you."*

Again, it is written, *"How much more shall the blood of Christ, who through the eternal Spirit offered Himself without spot to God, purge your conscience from the dead works to serve the living God" (Hebrews 9:14).*

The temptation of our Lord Jesus was very, very real. His total victory depended upon the Holy Spirit. This is brought out perfectly in the triumphant *words, "And Jesus returned in the power of the Spirit!" (Luke 4:14).* He had to have that source of power to overcome the evil one.

Now, in looking at all the previous scriptures, we mustn't overlook the words of John, when he was inspired to write, *"But Jesus did not commit Himself unto them, because He knew all men, and needed not that any should testify of man; for He knew what was in man" (John 2:24, 25).*

He knew, saw, acted and was moved by the Spirit of the Lord which was mightily upon Him.

What did Jesus say when He saw Nathanael? *"Before Philip called thee, when thou wast under the fig tree, I saw thee."*

Nathanael immediately responded with the cry, "Oh, Rabbi, you're the Son of God! You're the King of Israel!"

And Jesus replied and said literally, "Ah Nathanael, you're saying that because I said I saw you under the fig tree. But you haven't seen anything yet!"

Jesus saw by the eye of the Spirit. Nathanael saw by human intellect, and there is a vast difference between the two.

Jesus, weary from His journey in the dusty, dry land and searing heat, paused at the well of Samaria. There was a woman there who was of mixed blood, a Samaritan. Another Jew would have despised her, for she had Jewish blood in her veins, mixed with the blood of Gentiles. Even her doctrine was wrong, for it was part truth, part error.

She gave Jesus a drink of water and He began to draw her into conversation, promising her water that would forever quench her thirst. Then He made reference to her husband. Shock waves must have rolled through her nervous system as those piercing eyes looked into her life and left "all things naked and opened unto the eyes of Him with whom we have to do." *"I have no husband,"* she replied through dry lips.

"In this thing you are telling the truth," Jesus told her. *"You have had five husbands and the man you live with now is not your husband."*

Yet the words of Jesus did not condemn; He simply had told her a truth that He could not have known except the Holy Spirit imparted that truth to Him. Therefore, although His words brought strong conviction, they also brought great joy to her heart. She ran back into the city and told everyone to come and see "a man who told me all that ever I did." And the result was a revival in that city.

Jesus went alone into the mountains to pray, but His inner eyes never left His disciples who were attempting to cross the Sea of Galilee, that body of water where storms can sweep in so quickly.

194

He saw His friends struggling against the tossing waves and the fierce winds, and He left the place of prayer to go to their aid.

An evangelist whom I know slightly was driving along the highway somewhere in California, when he was strongly moved upon to get off the highway and follow the direction of the Spirit's leading. He did so. Mysteriously he was led to a mental hospital. The Lord dropped a name into his heart. He went into the hospital and asked to see the woman with that name. A few minutes later he stood at the foot of a bed where she lay in torment.

As this man in his late thirties or early forties began to speak with her, he discovered that she had once walked with God. But the enemy of her soul had come in with such vicious lies that she had broken under the load. The end result was that she had had to be institutionalized.

The evangelist spoke to her about resisting the devil, not with her own human intellect which only leads to failure, but with the Word of God. That and that alone. Then he laid hands on her and prayed. God gave the woman a miracle of deliverance and she was discharged from the hospital and sent home. God had sent this man supernaturally with a simple and profound message of, "Thus saith the Lord," and the work was complete.

A. W. Tozer says that Jesus was not only God with man, but He was man with God. He knows and understands every circumstance, every situation in our lives. If we are but sensitive to His Spirit, He will work miracles and move mountains through us.

We continually look at time, measuring it off by a piece of paper called a calendar; but God looks beyond time into eternity, and He is trying to get us ready to live in eternity. We were never designed or destined for the boundaries of earth. God never planned for us to live on the lowlands of spiritual living. We were made for the skies, designed for heaven. And so God moves upon and through us, perfecting, molding, tearing and binding up.

In *Mark 2:18* we read that Jesus "knew their thoughts", but David went a step further. He wrote the tender words; "He knows our frame; He remembers that we are dust." Thank God for that!

Aren't you glad that He knows all about you, and that there need never be a secret from Him who understands all? He knows it all, but He knows that we know only in part. He knows that we cannot operate, mature or force our way into the Spirit. He who gives spiritual gifts to men and women must be responsible to perfect them. How great He is, and how fluttering and floundering our best is unless He helps.

Surely, we can exclaim with Mark; *"What manner of man is this?"* What manner of man? He was the God-man (but still totally man), anointed and empowered by the Holy Spirit. And what is His promise to us? It is remarkably the same. *"But ye shall receive power, after that the Holy Ghost is come upon you" (Acts 1:8).*

Chapter Eight

WORDS ARE CREATIVE

I have strung words together like links in a chain since I was eight years old. I was given a toy typewriter for Christmas, the old kind that had a big round dial with the letters of the alphabet on it. You dialed the letter and poked the round dial and a weak-looking, rather tired letter popped out onto the paper. I called it the 'dial and poke' system of typing. Slow, badly done and scarcely legible, I was none-the-less released when all the pent-up words were on the paper. Sometimes I stayed up until 2:30 a.m. pecking away — if I could swing it without my parents knowing it!

So, I know something of the power of words. I know, for example, that the lead character in any book or story must be liked by the reader, even if he happens to be a scoundrel. I know that I have the power, through words, to make my reader happy or sad, give him hope or despair, cause him to quit or to try again. With words a writer can challenge his or her reader to tithe, witness or make a total commitment to Christ. Words are truly POWER-full!

The Bible says that the power of life and death are in the tongue. No wonder the tongue, though the smallest member of the body, is the most difficult to control and is the one the Holy Spirit seeks to conquer. It is the last part of us to surrender when we receive the baptism in the Holy Spirit, and yet often afterwards finds itself again in gossiping and tale-bearing. The tongue can cut and divide another Christian or a whole church. Words can build up, tear down, bless or curse.

We've all heard someone say, "If only I could take back the words I said!" Or, "I could have bit off my tongue!"

Too late we realize that once we have spoken, the words we have said will live on forever. Someone will hear the ring of our words, whether for good or for bad, for the rest of his life. Bitter words, angry words, words of hate and rebellion. The results are wounded hearts, crushed spirits, lives lived out in despair. The words we speak are creative words.

God spoke the worlds into being and holds them there by the word of His power. *Hebrews 1:3* This is verified again in *2 Peter 3, verses 5, 6 and 7, ". . . that by the word of God the heavens were of old, and the earth standing out of the water and in the water, by which the world then being overflowed with water, perished. But the heavens and the earth which are now, by the same word are kept in store . . . ."*

God spoke. And it was so. His words were creative.

Jesus spoke in the synagogue and a withered hand was made whole. He spoke and demons tore their victims and came forth, unable to hold their ground under the power of His words. He spoke and lepers were cleansed, the blind could see, cripples walked, the deaf heard and the dumb spoke.

This particular writing is at a much later date than at the beginning of the book, and I can say that last Sunday — just slightly over a week ago — on the island of Kauai, Hawaii, in a little town you could miss seeing if you closed your eyes for a moment, I saw a crippled finger release and straighten. It was made perfectly whole as the others through simply commanding it to be healed.

But let's go on a step further now, into creative words produced by the word of knowledge.

Look again at Elisha in the healing of Namaan the leper. When Elisha's servant Gehazi went after Namaan's chariot and accepted those gifts which Elisha had already rejected, the man Elisha knew exactly what his servant was up to. There was a confrontation when Gehazi returned and Elisha spoke to his servant by the word of knowledge what he had done. Then the prophet Elisha simply commanded by words that the leprosy that had been upon Namaan come upon Gehazi, and that word became creative. Gehazi went out from the presence of Elisha a leper 'as white as snow'.

A man by the name of Jairus came and fell down before our Lord Jesus, pleading with Him to come and lay hands on his sick child that she might not die.

While Jesus was accompanying the man a great crowd pressed upon Him, slowing His progress. An unseen woman, evidently crawling through the dirt and grime and smell of human bodies, reached out a trembling hand to touch the hem of Jesus' garment. That very instant Jesus felt strength, or power, go out of Him. He stopped and asked who touched Him. His disciples, who often came up with wrong answers, chided Him because so many were pressing against and touching Him. But He said in effect, "No, no, you don't understand. This touch was different." And the woman fell before Him, confessing what she had done. Then He spoke to her that she could go in peace, for she was healed.

A messenger came running up to the crowd, shouting that it was too late. The daughter of Jairus was already dead. There was no more need to trouble the Master of men.

But Jesus knew something different. He knew that she was not actually dead. Yet a moment before He had not known who the person was who had touched Him. A seeming paradox, except that again we must realize that this mighty God-man, Jesus, was dependent upon the Holy Spirit for all that He did. And the Holy Spirit was making Him to know that this child was not dead, though from every indication it was so.

Jesus gave Jairus a word of encouragement, asking the man to trust Him. And when they reached his home, the wailers had already begun their noisy commotion. Weeping was loud and profuse. Jesus put them all aside and took with Him only His three disciples and the child's parents, then went into the sick room.

Taking the child by the hand, He gave a gentle command to the twelve-year-old girl to get up. She immediately did so.

First, He knew that she was not really dead. Not in the sense that the people thought, at least. Secondly, He acted upon what He knew. Thirdly, He spoke out of the knowledge within. The results were creative and instantaneous.

Another time a centurion, a man with great authority, came to Jesus on behalf of a sick child. But he insisted that he was not worthy to have Christ come into his home. If He would but speak the word, the child would be healed. This also shows the power of words, but lacks the inner knowledge as accounted in the previous story.

Four men lowered a paralyzed friend through the roof where Jesus was preaching. Jesus saw how much they believed and told the sick man that his sins were forgiven him. (This, in other ministries, could be related with other accounts given in this book of a sickness being prayed for that the person didn't know he had and then told he'd been healed.) We know that Jesus didn't work that way, but He did so far as the Jewish religious leaders were concerned.

They laughed Him to scorn. Anyone could tell a person his sins were forgiven! Furthermore, they accused Jesus of speaking blasphemy, for who but God could forgive sin?

And Jesus knew their thoughts. Knowledge! And out of that deep-seated inner knowledge, He spoke. Here's what He said,

Why reason ye these things in your hearts? Which is easier to say to the sick of the palsy, Thy sins are forgiven thee; or to say, Arise, and take up thy bed, and walk? But that ye may know that the Son of man hath authority on earth to forgive sins [He saith to the sick of the palsy], I say unto thee, Arise, and take up thy bed, and go thy way into thine house.

Beyond a doubt, the Jewish leaders were already quaking at the burning realization that Jesus had read their thoughts. But now, to see His words create a miracle before their very eyes. In the modern vernacular, I'm sure they couldn't get it all together.

Jesus often stunned the intellect of various folk, even His own disciples. And out of His interior knowledge there sprang, not always physical healings, but sometimes a gentle rebuke, sometimes prayer.

He knew, for instance about the deep and bitter experience of Peter's denial before it happened and warned Peter of what was about to take place. But with the warning came also the promise to pray that Peter's faith would not fail.

But, you say, give us some today experiences. There are plenty of them springing out of many ministries in this great day we are living in.

One of the first times I recall seeing the word "heal" without prayer or the laying on of hands was in Bell Gardens, California. A Catholic man had refused to come to the meeting to hear a lady preacher. His Lutheran wife came regularly, and finally at the beginning of the next week she persuaded him to come to a service with her.

Before I came on the platform I was suddenly struck by a jabbing pain in my left hip. It was not my pain. I was not, nor am I now, troubled by such an affliction. Gently the Holy Spirit urged me to call it out.

Oh, if we could but get used to the idea, catch the revelation that the Holy Spirit is not an influence, or a power, or an invisible vapor that sort of floats around to convict of sin and, in general help or bless people. He is infinitely more than that! May I say that more and more I find myself talking to the Holy Spirit, to move and work with me when in ministry, to guide me and use me when I am at home, to make Himself known to me as a very real and wonderful person.

Many go so far as to think of Him as a personality but not really as a Person! He is a Person! He deposits His glory and power into our lives, then sets about to so move and live through us as to best use that deposit of power. And when you are filled with the Spirit, He fills every part and portion of your body. He fits you perfectly, for He is poured into you. If you are tall and skinny or short and fat, He will perfectly fit you, and you can feel Him move and stir in every part of you.

He perfectly knows how to pray through you, for He alone perfectly knows the will of God. Jesus went away and sent the Spirit back to us not only as His supreme representative but as His co-equal.

If we could but see the need — our need — of the Spirit's presence in us in whatever work we undertake for God. Oh, the wealth, the perfect source of all knowledge, wisdom, faith, power!

We should learn to talk with the Holy Spirit, to work with Him, to know Him as we know the Father and the Son.

The Holy Spirit is a tremendous personality. He hears, He sees, He feels and can be grieved, resisted and quenched. He guides and yet will go before us in ministry to work and prepare hearts. How much more we would be used of God if we could but see that the Holy Spirit is a wonderful Person Jesus has given us to help us in our work for Him.

That was a short side excursion, but I trust it was profitable.

I had suffered with a chronic colitis for long years, sometimes having as many as two severe attacks daily. Occasionally the doctor would have to come to the house to give me an injection for the pain. Other times I landed in hospitals, receiving injections that would put me to sleep until the spasm stopped.

Through the years I grew much worse. Life was wretched for me and filled with pain. Many times I was struck while eating and got to the place where I feared going out with friends to eat.

A minister was coming to Tucson, where we lived at that time, to have a night's meeting in a men's club building. I said, "Lord, if this is Your night for me to be healed, would You show this man my need?"

I was sitting in the front row at the meeting that night. In the preliminary part of the service, while we were worshipping and singing choruses, the man walked past me and suddenly stopped. He looked at me strangely. Everything within me leaped forward with anticipation. I knew that God was answering my prayer. Faith rose high within my heart.

"Why, sister," he said, "I see you all doubled up with pain."

Then he began to perfectly describe my condition. I began to weep as the Spirit of God came upon me. And from that moment to this present day, some fourteen years later, I have been perfectly healed.

I stood in the pulpit in Modesto, California ministering the Word, when that Word was suddenly interrupted by a sparkling silver upper spine that appeared before me. Automatically I paused to call it out. A man answered instantly that he was the one, and he was perfectly healed.

This spoken word that springs out of inner knowledge is different from the written Word of God. It's a living, creative force, the living word! The Logos, or written Word is one thing, but when it becomes alive to us, quickening us and making us whole and alive, it becomes the Rhema, the living word.

Madame Guyon said that the eternal Word when communicated to a soul is something the Devil cannot counterfeit.

Chapter Nine

IT IS COMPATIBLE

Yes, it is wholly compatible with the other gifts of the Spirit. We have seen this with the various types of divine or 'spiritual' healings wrought through the word of knowledge. We have seen how it inter-relates with revelation, how it creates, and how it sees beyond the facade of life into the interior bruisings and crushings in order to bring inner healings.

In following chapters, we shall see how the word of knowledge inter-relates with the gift of discerning of spirits — to such a degree that at times it is nearly impossible to tell one from the other.

For a moment let's touch on the compatibility of the working of the word of knowledge with personal prophecy. And let's be crystal clear of the ground upon which we stand before entering into this delicate subject.

Personal prophecy is absolutely Scriptural, and let us never believe otherwise. If there are doubts in your mind about this, then, before moving on in this chapter, take your Bible in hand and see for yourself that it is in the Bible. Look at all the Old Testament prophets. Not merely the ones who wrote the Scriptures prophetically as they were moved upon by the Holy Spirit, but those men and women of God who prophesied. In the Old Testament men of God prophesied to individuals.

Isaac prophesied to Jacob, Moses to Pharoah. Samuel prophesied to Saul, Elijah to Elisha. Plus, a host of other personal prophesies that can be dug out of the Old Testament.

In the New Testament Elizabeth prophesied to Mary, Zacarias to those present at the birth of John the Baptist. Paul prophesied to Timothy. The daughters of Philip were prophetesses. Other women prophesied, Deborah, Huldah, Miriam. Anna prophesied when Jesus was taken to the temple as a baby; and so did a man by the name of Simeon. Ananias laid hands on Paul while Paul was yet blind and prophesied over him.

However, and I use that word strongly, personal prophecy was never overdone in the Scriptures, and it should not be overdone today. (Needless to say, there are those in our ranks in the NOW outpouring of the Spirit who are grossly misusing, or over-using, this gift.) But in every case, the strongest perhaps being the case of Saul coming into the city to look for a word from a seer, the Lord having already revealed to Samuel what was going to take place — knowledge worked first, then out of that knowledge came the personal prophecy.

Let's take a bird's-eye view at it:

Saul's father had sent his son to look for some lost donkeys. He went and looked through the hill country but could not find them. Finally, Saul told his servant that they must turn back because his father might become worried about them too. Then he spoke these words, ". . . *there is in this city a man of God, and he is an honorable man; all that he saith cometh surely to pass: now, let us go there; perhaps he can show us the way that we should go"* (I Samuel 9:6).

Some young maidens told the man where Samuel could be found and they started to him. They had not known that the day before the Lord had spoken to Samuel that Saul would be coming to see him. God had been specific about the time of day he would come and from what tribe he would come. Then the Lord had appointed Samuel to anoint Saul to be captain over the people of Israel, and to save Israel from the Philistines.

Saul came face to face with Samuel and asked the question, *"Where is the seer?"* Samuel replied, *"I am the seer."* Then came the startling words, *"As for thine asses that were lost three days ago, set not thy mind on them; for they are found"* (I Samuel 9:20).

Do you see how great God is? How infinitely mindful and how practical, too, with the issues of life. God was thinking primarily of His chosen people Israel and the man He wished to use to free His people. Yet, He did not forget the smallest matter, and that was the donkeys. God remembered the donkeys. Probably, He allowed the donkeys to become lost in the first place so Saul would be at the appointed place at the appointed time.

Later on, in the following chapter, Samuel anointed Saul and prophesied to him of what the Lord wanted. In *verse 6* we read these powerful words, *"And the Spirit of the Lord shall come upon thee, and thou shalt prophecy with them, and shalt be turned into another man."*

That verse is still literally true today for every single person who will take it, clasp it to them and claim it!

I have had personal prophecy given to me many, many times — as in the case of Fran whom I mentioned earlier. Another woman has tried unsuccessfully through the years to prophecy to me. Her letters have come to me through the past five years. False personal prophecies, one thing after another. Very personal issues regarding my children, my ministry and my walk with God. Then she wrote that I have two friends whom she described to perfection. She said they were tearing down me and my ministry.

I laughed. These two friends are the two who hold me up the most strongly.

But it's no laughing matter in reality. God has much to say in the Word about the prophets who prophecy lies and say, *"God saith"* (Ezek. 13:17; Deut. 18:21, 22; Jer. 23:16-31). A true prophecy whether personal or otherwise will absolutely follow this pattern, *"The prophet who prophesieth of peace, when the word of the prophet shall come to pass, then shall the prophet be known, that the Lord hath truly sent him."*

Many is the young zealous Christian who has gone out into some form of ministry because someone prophesied it to him and he tried to make it happen. The results were shipwreck, and, in some cases, a total disfellowshipping with God.

For Jesus' sake and your own, if someone should come along and tell you to go to Africa as missionary, don't go! If you do and God is not in it, you will be apt to end up in a cannibal's pot somewhere.

If someone gives you a personal prophecy, don't do anything. Wait. You have nothing to worry about; for with God there is never any pressure, struggle or conflict. If He was in that word of prophecy, He will most certainly bring it to pass. If He was not in it, you have been both wise and safe to wait.

True personal prophecy springs out of knowledge or revelation. The word of knowledge is so compatible with it that at times it may seem to be one and the same gift.

Other personal prophecies came my way, prophecies that have absolutely confirmed what God had already told me. I really like that. I believe that God works on both ends of the line. If God has told me something and then someone comes along and tells

208

me by way of personal prophecy what God has already said, then I can say "Praise the Lord! He has confirmed His word to me."

But I still wait, I never try to make it happen. God showed me years ago the reality of *Acts 10:38* and I began to pray, not only for the anointing of the Spirit, but for the anointing of power. God promised it to me.

A minister who did not know me, the same one under whose ministry in the word of knowledge I was healed of severe, chronic colitis told me that the power of God was going to come into my hands for ministry. It did and does wherever I minister. This same man prophesied that the word of knowledge would come into me and I would know supernaturally by the Spirit. It happened.

But, you see, the difference is that God had already told me and the prophecy was simply a confirmation. Then, in due time, God began to open doors and continues to open doors of ministry today ten years later, without my help.

I suppose that I have used personal prophecy maybe five times in the whole of my ministry. I just don't see it being used that much in the Bible, particularly in the New Testament. If it was not over-used in that day, should it be over-used today? In many circles it is. Sometimes when the denominations receive the baptism in the Holy Spirit, they go off in little groups and begin to prophecy to each other, and many times it brings confusion, disillusionment and even a loss of faith.

It can be a precious thing, personal prophecy, but it's much greater if we let the Lord lead our lives and allow someone to confirm it, should the Lord so move.

During the most difficult year of my ministry, three different persons in different parts of the country prophesied to me. Each person said exactly the same thing, almost word for word. God had seen my discouragement, very extreme, and sent His word through willing messengers to cheer and encourage my heart.

Once when I was conducting a revival in a certain city in California, I was confronted by a young girl in the prayer line. This girl, whom we shall call Gail, was about to marry a hippie. It seemed as though he had cast a spell over her, and, though he treated her roughly and stayed out nights with other girls, she was desperately in love with him. She wanted God's best, and she was groping for a decision. The young man in question was on drugs and was a known warlock. Sometimes at night his face would come floating to her through the darkness of her room in a blue mist.

God gave me knowledge and a mental picture. Words formed upon my lips. The Spirit said through me in part, "Gail, if you marry this young man, you will either commit suicide or fight the desire to commit suicide within three months." There was more, but that was the gist of it.

She married him in December, a beautiful young Christian who was enchanted with this boy in witchcraft and drugs. Within a month the prophecy began to come true. Living in a tiny, depressing apartment several stories above a swimming pool, with other addicts and occult members, the powers of darkness sweeping at her very soul, she stood and dreamed over and over of plunging over the edge and into the ground below. Ending it all. This haunting desire to commit suicide did not leave until the three months were up. Her life was saved through a faithful mother who came whenever she was called and stood by in prayer.

Sometimes it takes God years to fulfill a prophecy. Remember, He never hurries. But He is never late. He prepares the vessel well before He sends it forth or uses it much in ministry.

210

I know people who live their lives in looking 'for a word' from others. It seems they do not know how to draw the water of salvation for themselves, to literally, *"Drink waters out of thine own cistern, and running waters out of thine own well," (Proverbs 5:15)* but must always be drinking from someone else's life. This is not the will of God for any of His children. He wants us to find His will for ourselves, and He is so willing to work with us if we will only learn to linger in that divine Presence until He comes and speaks to us afresh. Then we need not always seek a word from someone else for our lives.

How is it, then? Personal prophecy is good if it confirms something God has already revealed to your heart. It must line up with the Scriptures, it must bear up to circumstances, and it must bear record in our own hearts. It will edify (strengthen), exhort (advise or challenge) and it will comfort (impart hope).

It will never rob you of your joy, or bring depression, discouragement, judgement or condemnation. It is not silly things like, "Thou shalt give up thy pant suits and thy Pepsi colas." Yes, that one really did happen. Prophecy was used by the human spirit as a conveyance in getting a message across. And the fever of the human spirit can be a devastating and devouring force when it is not fully submitted and yielded to the Holy Spirit and under His complete control.

An elderly man came through the city where I lived and made his way into a fellowship where the Spirit had been graciously outpoured. He announced the fact that he was being sent by the spirit to go through the country, selecting certain women who were to bear his children. 'Holy' children, he called them. And some women, unversed in the Word, were so gullible that they had an affair with this old man.

211

You say, "How in the world could anyone be stupid enough to do such a thing?"

I really don't know. Except that I do know this happened. And out of that same fellowship where, literally, the blind were trying to lead the blind, another man came and took some of the people into a desert where they were 'supposed to wait, as one big happy family, for Jesus to come'. Free love was what it amounted to, and many people whom I know personally escaped that snare and have beautiful ministries today.

Self-styled, self-imposed prophets who need desperately to be taught before they try to teach others.

Let it be said again that personal prophecy is a lovely gift and should be handled with skill under the direction of the Holy Spirit. If it lines up with the Word, if it confirms something God has shown you, if it bears with the situation around you, accept it as a confirmation from the Lord. But never, never try to make it happen. God will do that in His own good time.

Chapter Ten

AS RELATING TO
DISCERNING OF SPIRITS

There is an exceptionally fine line drawn between the gifts of the word of knowledge and the gift of discerning of spirits. Both are gifts of revelation and, being in the very same category, it is sometimes almost impossible to know whether if it is one gift in operation or the other. Indeed, they can work together so simultaneously so that they appear to be one and the same gift flowing. I always think of these two particular gifts as "Siamese twins." Let me illustrate.

I was not yet called of God into a ministry. Preparation stages had begun, though I wasn't aware of it at the time. I was aware of the fact that I was in the school of the Spirit, but I didn't know why.

After an evening service a young Baptist brother came to me and said, "Betty, there's a twelve-year-old girl back here who needs prayer. Would you meet me in the pastor's study and agree with me in prayer for her?"

"Of course, Larry." I followed my friend down the aisle and into the pastor's study, where I was immediately confronted by a cringing, stringy-haired wisp of a girl who was staring unseeingly into the shag carpet.

Instantly I knew something was wrong. A wrong spirit. A wrong life situation. Bitterness and hate fairly permeated that pastor's study. Knowledge. But it was knowledge coupled with and inter-related to discerning of spirits. The two gifts were inseparable.

Gently I tried to cup her face in my hands and lift her head so she could see me through that brown mop that looked more like seaweed than it did hair.

But the little girl cowed away from me, twisting so I could not look into her eyes. Now remember that the eyes are the windows of the soul. Sometimes oppression, when it is heavy enough, can be seen in the eyes. Most certainly, then, possession is clearly evident in the eyes of the victim.

The enemy, knowing this, will try every trick known to avoid looking into the eyes of any person who knows the spirits. The reason is simple enough. Once knowledge comes and there is a penetration into the enemy's territory, he knows he is discovered and therefore may lose his captive to God.

Always remember that the gifts of revelation probe the enemy's stronghold and disclose what he is doing. Is it any wonder, then, why Satan gets to the new Christian and much more to the individual newly filled with the Spirit before he can grow up into God and begin maturing in the things of God? The devil never knows where the attack will strike, nor who God may be preparing in the secret places for penetration into these dark areas by the gifts of revelation. Satan's purpose is to get to that potentially-power-filled believer and stop him where he is.

Suddenly, like a cascade of truth, like a swift breaker rolling upon a beach, like Niagra pitching itself mercilessly over the cliffs, the Holy Spirit was probing accurately into the child's life.

"You have a brother, don't you?"

214

She uncoiled her body like a serpent, and those blazing hate-filled eyes glared at me. "Yes!" The word was hissed out with all the pent-up poison of her soul.

"He has forced you to give him your body many times."

"Yes!"

"This brother of yours is eighteen years old."

"Almost." She trembled violently. "How — who told you?"

"The Lord." I pulled her to me gently. Larry was standing silently, head bowed praying. "He also tells me that your mother has deserted you and that you are now living with a woman who is not your mother."

Again, her body began to writhe and twist like a reptile coiling for the strike. Her head lowered and her gaze flashed away from mine. Such a mixture of evil spirits poured from this girl that both Larry and I were appalled. She was only twelve years of age! What terrible thing had driven her to such darkness?

But the Holy Spirit, faithful to the end, began once again to illuminate. The situation seemed to continually fluctuate between the word of knowledge and discerning of spirits. For, you see, they were working hand in hand. Knowledge spotlighted the cause, discerning of spirits the result. At that moment knowledge flooded in once more.

The mother of this girl had deserted her at an early age. The girl could not forgive her mother for that. She loathed her. To further frustrate and confuse her life, the brother she had sought to lean upon had let her down. Driven by loneliness and hate, another woman took her in. This woman was a lesbian.

The horror of it. It seemed nearly inconceivable. Let down by two women, used sexually by one woman and her blood brother, deserted by both father and mother, the child's life had become filled with demonic forces. But she wanted to be free.

And to this end we prayed. The child appeared to receive a great release, but neither Larry nor myself were able to keep track of her, and to this day we don't know what happened to her.

You can see, then, how the word of knowledge can so inter-relate with the gift of discerning of spirits that it is nearly impossible to tell the one from the other.

Sometimes the presence of a wrong spirit can cause one to become sick to their stomach. Other times there may be a penetration as though invisible rays are coming at you. Still other times it is possible to begin experiencing what the other person is experiencing.

A Lutheran friend of mine had company come into her home. Suddenly and without any provocation, she began to feel hate and anger. She was aghast, for these things are definitely not a part of her nature. And then she realized that one of the individuals who had entered her home was full of anger and hate Some would call these bad "vibes".

At any rate, when one is sensitive to the Holy Spirit, that same person will be sensitive to other spirits and can 'pick up' on other persons without really meaning to or wanting to. Certainly without trying to! It would make all of us to be alert to those things coming at us from other people and not become trapped into thinking these things have entered into our own hearts. (Watchman Nee's "Release of the Spirit" is excellent teaching along this line.)

In Colorado where I was conducting a meeting among the Nazarenes, I happened to meet a woman, quite unsaved, in a trailer park. Almost immediately something was wrong. Knowledge. In a very few minutes I began to be very nervous. I found it difficult to even look at this woman. I prayed, "Lord, what in the world is the matter with me? I wasn't nervous five minutes ago!" Then He showed me that this woman had a very nervous spirit and I was feeling what she was experiencing. That proved to be entirely true.

As it is true of the word of knowledge, it is also true of discerning of spirits, that the devil will say to you, "You should feel terrible, thinking thoughts like that about that person!" Or, "Careful now. You're judging, and you know what the Bible says about judging."

But again, it is as true of this gift as the other that when you know, you know and you know that you know! You can't help it. You don't go around trying to smell out a wrong spirit. You don't attempt to "read" people. You don't have to. If it's there, you know it. That's simple enough.

Personally, I can't bear being "read". I call it being "peopled."

One time during a hard rain storm late in the afternoon a knock came on my door. We lived up in the foothills out of Tucson, Arizona, and there stood a couple I did not know but who said they had attended the same Bible College I had attended. They came inside, took off their coats, sat down at the breakfast bar and watched me silently while I finished the evening meal. It was eerie. I didn't like it. I scarcely knew the couple and certainly disliked the idea of them coming in to eye me.

If there is a pure gift flowing from a life, that person does not have to try and make it work. The Holy Spirit and He alone governs that gift and causes it to operate. Therefore, it is effortless, flowing and free.

Kathryn Kuhlman said over and over again how surprised she was when the Holy Spirit moved, for He came sweeping in unexpectedly and began performing miracles. She might try to form a pattern of His working with her human intellect and He would swiftly change course and do it a different way.

217

In the final analysis, He moved sovereignly as He willed to move and left even Kathryn wondering and awed at how He did it. She knew and knew well that she had nothing to do with the miracles.

So it is. A true gift moves. It works. It stymies the individuals through whom it works. It is so that no one can put God in a box and say, "This is how it is done."

A man was leading the singing in a certain church. I had seen this man one time before and the same word leaped into my spirit for the man that had come unbidden to me in the opening chapter of this book. Phony. Deceptive.

A friend attended church with me on a Sunday night. The man of whom we are now speaking was again leading the singing. I knew my friend had great discernment, but I said nothing. We simply exchanged quick glances and took our seats.

My friend whispered "Oh no!" Knowledge.

"What is it?" I asked.

"I'm not sure, but it's really bad."

I talked to the Lord about it for a while. "He is in deception," I told her.

Now, everything he did was right. Everything he said was right. But he had a religious (deceptive, phony) spirit.

He finished the last song and took a seat in the congregation. A testimony service began, a time of sharing. He was the first one on his feet. He said, "I thank God that I am not in deception. I thank the Lord that I am on the right path and that my life is right with Him."

I said to my friend, "Well, the devil knows that we know."

Paul had a certain damsel who followed him around for three days. He knew she had a divining spirit (counterfeit for the word of

218

knowledge). He knew it. Yet he put up with it for three days. The knowledge he had penetrated into her life to know that her masters made money from her fortune-telling spirit, and Paul knew what the spirit was that she had. Everything she said was right. What she did was, seemingly, right. After all, she was following the Apostle Paul around telling everyone that he was a man of God and the people should listen to his message. But she was as phony as a three-dollar bill. Paul finally exposed her and commanded the spirit of divination to come out of her.

This glorious, sweeping stream of the Holy Spirit in our day is the greatest thing we could get caught up in. The Charismatics offer freshness, Calvary love, faith and a holy contagious excitement. Oh, that this love and zeal would sweep into every church across our nation and around the world, embracing every tongue, church, fellowship, nation and continent! That every barrier would bend and break to make way for pure, sweet Calvary love to flow over the walls we have built around ourselves and our little cliques! That the sweet inner reality of Jesus would permeate every heart and the Holy Spirit would be utterly free to take the things of God and show them to us!

With every atom of my being, I am in and for the charismatic move. I want to wade out into the depths of that pure flowing stream and lose myself so that only my head will be seen — and my head is Jesus Christ!

But with all the glow and the wonder of this move upon the earth, there are also danger points. Satan will always see to that. And one of the danger points is the self-styled demon-chaser. There is at least one in every group, and sometimes there are two or three. They have people coming to their homes all hours of the day and night, totally caught up with the bizarre thrill of casting demons out of people.

There are authentic cases, we know that. But they are not as many, perhaps, as some would have us to believe. I once heard a man preaching about 'popcorn demons', and I thought, 'Oh, this is just too much!" A man likes popcorn and eats it in the evenings while he is relaxing after a hard day's work and this man says he has a popcorn demon. So, one could make a demon out of everything, I suppose. But souls can be wounded, sometimes beyond repair because of untaught persons seeking to teach others the way of deliverance.

One denominational couple in my city became such self-appointed demon-caster-outers. And many were the people who walked away from their home and from the baptism in the Holy Spirit because of what they learned in that foothill home. One such couple was a Dutch Reformed minister and his wife, sound and solid folk who had been filled with the Spirit and were ablaze with the glory of God. They met the other couple at a breakfast and were invited to their home. Then, the minister's wife was told to sit in a chair near a door. She was asked the question, "All right, how many demons do you have?"

The minister's wife had not the foggiest notion of what the man was talking about. She knew nothing about demons; she just knew that she'd discovered 'the treasure hidden in a field' and it was glorious. But she was on the hot seat. They were waiting for her to reply. Finally, in a small voice, she said, "Six." (Later she told me she could have said sixty-six, it was all the same to her.)

Whereupon the man opened the door and told the demons to get out. That was enough trauma, but that was not the end of the story. For months this minister's wife, who had now become a close friend, was being dogged, harassed, oppressed by the enemy of her soul day and night. It took a real anointing and much

220

counselling, but she is free today and she and her husband are serving the Lord in a very beautiful way.

Others were not so fortunate. Denominational ministers found their way to this home — and out again. Disillusioned, turned off, they wanted no part in what they saw going on there. If that was a part of the baptism of the Holy Spirit, forget it.

I could go on and on in this chapter. I could tell you about a man who came into a prayer line once in California. He had a severe problem in his neck. God did not heal him. The word of knowledge began to flow, but it was coupled distinctly with the gift of discerning of spirits.

"You actually are obsessed by a demon of hate. This hate is directed to someone close to you. When you get rid of the hate, you will be healed."

I was stunned. I heard the words, but it was hard to believe that they were coming from my lips. I felt like an innocent bystander listening in on someone else's conversation. But the faith that it was accurate was absolute.

He stared. His mouth dropped open. "I - I do," he stammered. "I really do. I hate my daughter-in-law!"

"Then let's agree and bind this thing and loose love to her. Then you come back into the prayer line and God will heal you.'

He was back in the line two nights later. His daughter-in-law had come to the house for a while and he felt genuine love pouring out to her. Of course, you guessed it already! He was healed in his neck that very night

Oh, there are so many pathetic cases. Cases of bondage. Is it any wonder that God inspired the words in *Isaiah*, *"Is this not the fast that I have chosen? to loose the bands of wickedness, to undo the heavy burdens, and to let the oppressed go free, that ye break every yoke?" (Isaiah 58:6).*

Sometimes there are conditions to be met. Other times God simply moves sovereignly by His Spirit. But one thing is sure: He desires that His people are free and at rest. And how do people get themselves into such terrible situations? I don't know.

Never shall I forget the 'pig woman' my youngest daughter and met while taking a short rest on a farm in Missouri. The woman who was our hostess during this time wanted to show us around their farm. It was a little bit difficult, because we were definitely in pig country, and all one had to do to be convinced of that fact was to take a deep breath!

'I want to take you by to see a woman who really needs help," our hostess said. And, while I wasn't too keen about visiting anyone on that particular day, I wanted to be agreeable. So, we parked in front of this small white frame house, very unpretentious, and knocked at the door.

The man who came to the door was old and bent with age. He asked us to come inside and hobbled with us toward the bedroom where his wife lay, too ill to be on her feet. As a matter of fact, we discovered that she had been lying on her side for eight long years.

On the table beside her bed was a vast assortment of pills and bottles of liquid. I think I have never seen such an accumulation of drugs for any one person in my whole life.

No one needed special knowledge to see that something was dreadfully wrong. But both my daughter and I began to receive insight into the interior part of her. She was a registered nurse. She loved being doted to and cared for. In essence, she loved her Cherith too much to leave it.

She was the shape of a large hog. Her face had taken on the appearance of a hog. I suppose there must have been twenty or thirty pictures decking her walls of various kinds and sizes of pigs. Her lamps were ceramic pigs. Dozens of objects in her room were in some form of a pig. Her living room walls were covered with pictures of pigs, and in the dining room a China closet exhibited about five hundred salt and pepper shakers, pigs. There were literally thousands of them in the house. The woman in bed had, literally, the spirit of a pig. She was not looking for help or for healing but was content to stay there on her side — not on her back but on her side as a pig would lay — and have her husband wait on her.

Knowledge did not extend so far as to reveal why she had allowed herself to get into this condition, what inner bitternesses or bruisings, perhaps, had driven her so far. But that she was content with her condition was evident.

This particular chapter could go on almost forever, but it has to close somewhere so it might as well be here.

Much is to be said about the gift of discerning of spirits and whole volumes could be written about it, but it is sufficient to reiterate that we have been most interested here in showing how the gift of the word of knowledge relate and accurately zeros in to interrelate with the gift of discerning spirits.

Chapter Eleven

"IF TWO OF YOU SHALL AGREE"

Verily, I say unto you, Whatsoever ye shall bind on earth shall be bound in heaven: and whatsoever ye shall loose on earth shall be loosed in heaven. Again I say unto you that if two of you shall agree on earth as touching any thing that they shall ask, it shall be done for them of my father which is in heaven (Matt. 18:18, 19).

And then Jesus said in essence, "If two or three of you can truly agree on anything, I will be there with you."

Agreement is so important among God's people. It is in fact so vital to the Lord that He is many times hindered in working among us by our acute lack of agreeing. Over and over in the Word of God, there is the note of urgency in being of one mind, one spirit, submitting to one another's thoughts and intents. When a person finds another individual who can perfectly agree with him in prayer, believing, something is going to happen!

Always a great believer in being in one accord in prayer, it never even occurred to me that God could bring two souls into such union in prayer that a gift could operate through those two and operate in beautiful perfection.

224

I had witnessed an individual giving an interpretation to a tongue and falter in the middle of it and stop. Then another member of the body of Christ would take it up exactly where the other person broke off and finish the interpretation in a smooth and simple operation. This was beautiful too.

But one day, just prior to my going into a meeting in another state, a friend and I were in prayer for that series of meetings. Suddenly, to my amazement, my friend began to weep. A spirit of intercession had come upon her and she sobbed as though her heart would break. When she could speak, she told me about a woman who was going to be in that meeting. She told me about what the woman would look like, about how old she would be and said there was something, some tragedy or deep oppression upon her life.

But that wasn't all. She also saw a young man in the meeting and told me where he would be sitting. Outwardly he would appear perfectly confident and composed, but inwardly he was shattered.

Now my friend certainly was not going to be in that meeting. Neither had I ever experienced anything like this, where the word of knowledge could flow without interruption between two persons. I made mental notes but left the matter completely in the hands of God.

A few days later I arrived at the end of my destination. Sunday morning the meeting began. The flow of the Spirit was beautiful from the first moment; and before the Word could be given there was literally a divine explosion in that place.

Faith was in that church! Faith for healings, faith working with the word of knowledge, faith building, building! A man with a bad knee was instantly healed and went out under the power as though he had been struck by lightning. A young woman the greatest soul winner in the church — was also slain by the power of the Holy Spirit and healed instantly of a stomach disorder.

Then she was illuminated. The woman my friend had wept and prayed for. She was sitting on the middle aisle to my left about two thirds of the way back. There could be no doubt but that she was the one.

Faith seized hold of everyone. Boldness to declare what the Spirit was saying was so present that I was lifted outside of myself, standing there listening.

There was a series of circumstances in the life that had produced a gloom, a deep oppression, both mentally and spiritually. God wanted to strip away the depression like bark from a tree and give her new life, new joy, new strength! Oh, there was more, much more, but it's too long ago to remember it all.

The power of the Spirit settled upon her. Her face began to glow. We saw the Lord turn her mourning into dancing. We saw Him exchange her spirit of heaviness for a garment of praise. That night when she came back to the service, I didn't recognize her, so much had her whole countenance changed and her life transformed.

That morning while the Holy Spirit was brooding and hovering over His people, ministering to them and healing them, I had had an awareness of a young man sitting to my right on the very front seat. There was no sense of urgency regarding him, not even the nudge that he should be ministered to in the service. Yet somewhere away back in my spirit, I knew that he was the young man my friend had also seen, prayed for and wept over.

In the evening service, however, his wife and little boy were with him. Suddenly there was an illumination. Revelation.

Outwardly this young man was an aggressive, outgoing and, in general, a very happy-go-lucky kind of a guy. But it was only a facade. Inside it was quite another story. He was terrified, afraid of a thousand fears, cringing, crumbling. Their marriage was on extremely shaky ground and his wife was thinking of leaving him. He felt inadequate, inferior, incapable.

Walking toward the rear of the church and taking his hand, the Holy Spirit gave words that were whispered quietly into his ear. He crumpled like a piece of tissue paper which one could crumple with a hand. His face twisted with his inner agonies and he fell to the floor under the power Of God,

His young wife received ministry and their lives were turned around by the wisdom, knowledge and tenderness of God.

Never before or since that time have I ever seen the operation of the gift of the word of knowledge flow forth from two individuals so perfectly.

Just think — ! What if the whole body of Christ were so in one mind, one aim, purpose and desire to see the kingdom of God advance! The world would be changed overnight. No one would covet another's position in the course of spiritual world events. Each would fill his and her position and we would move forward with a single motive; that is to see this Gospel of the Kingdom preached around the globe for every nation, language and tribe to hear. Not worrying who is going to get the credit for casting out a devil or performing a miracle, but just moving on and flowing on together to see this great work accomplished for God.

Chapter Twelve

STRIVING FOR PERFECTION

A h, yes! Perfection. How can any one of us be perfect until "that which is perfect has come"? Paul admitted that he had not attained, but he was pressing toward the goal. And, as long as we are human beings, there are going to be mistakes and imperfections. But there can be a 'pressing into' or a 'pressing forward', striving toward God, waiting before Him. The gifts given to us by the Spirit can certainly become mature as we yield ourselves to Him and ourselves mature in Christ Jesus.

How very true it is that, *"Now we see through a glass darkly; but then, face to face; now I know in part, but then shall I know even as also I am known" (I Cor. 13:12).* And again, in *verses 9 and 10, "For we know in part, and we prophecy in part. But when that which is perfect is come, then that which is in part shall be done away."*

A minister in Nebraska asked, "Betty, what happened? I can't figure it out! It almost blew my mind! I knew this thing about someone and confronted her with it and she flat-out denied that it was true."

A minister in Arizona said, "What do you do with this one, Betty? I felt so sure the Lord had shown me something about someone that I went right down the line on it when she was in a prayer line one night. And it was absolutely wrong! I was so flabbergasted; I still haven't recovered from it."

A very young minister using this gift for personal exploitation got a man on stage, took away his cigarettes and stomped them into the fibers of the wooden floor and declared that the man would never have the desire to smoke another cigarette. The man stared at the evangelist and said calmly, "I will. I'll go out and buy another pack as soon as this service is over."

Not one to give up easily, the evangelist asked if the man was willing to say a prayer after him. The man was willing. The evangelist prayed something like this;

"Dear Jesus —"

"Dear J-Jesus," repeated the man, snickering.

"Take away this filthy cigarette habit!"

The man laughed softly. "Take away this filthy cigarette habit."

"And help me to give up my liquor."

"Help me to give up my liquor," the man repeated obediently.

"Don't let me even touch another bottle of whiskey."

The man aped him. "Don't let me ever touch another bottle of whiskey."

"Change my life completely."

Repeat: "Change my life completely."

The prayer ended and the evangelist threw his arm around the other man's shoulders. "Well, brother, you're going to be a changed man from now on. You have been a very heavy drinker, haven't you?"

The man was steady, facing the microphone. "No, I haven't."

The evangelist frowned. "Oh? But you've certainly had your drinking sprees, is that right?"

"The other man's expression remained unchanged. "No, that isn't right." The evangelist stared at the middle-aged man. "You mean you've only been a social drinker?"

"No, I don't ever drink at all."

To describe the succession of facial changes that took place on the face of that evangelist would be impossible, for they varied from shock to comedy. Finally, he slapped the man on the shoulders, shoved him off the platform and said meekly, "Well, praise God, brother, you never will either."

It was both comical and tragic. It was rancid. Really rancid.

God will never become impatient or grieved when individuals check the word of knowledge out a couple of times. What do I mean by that? Ask the Holy Spirit for a confirmation. Either He will bring the thing strongly to your remembrance again, you will become aware of the pain in your body again, or situations will swing just so that He brings you right back to the point of beginning, when the word of knowledge first came to you.

I was sitting in a congregation on a Sunday morning. God gave me a word of knowledge. Now, it wasn't my service, so it gets a little bit sticky here and we have to really ask God to make the proper opening if He wants the word to come forth.

The Lord gave the perfect opportunity. I gave the word. The word was that someone was suffering from pain in the right ear. The woman with the affliction stepped forward and I was given permission to pray for her. Did God heal that ear? He did not. He broke her smoking habit in a split second, after she had struggled with it for 47 years!

You say, "Why, that's remarkable!" I agree. But why didn't God give me a word about her cigarettes? I don't know why God does some of the things He does or why He does them the way He does them. Maybe she would have been terribly embarrassed if her cigarette habit had been called out. Maybe she would not have responded. I do not pretend to know the reason why. Maybe it was a deficiency on my part. One thing I know: I have a letter in my files received just recently from "Your non-smoking friend!" That was five years ago.

Oh, we are truly such imperfect people. And, while we are working with a perfect, omniscient, God, He is working through highly imperfect people who often take Him on side trips and detours. We often are not as sensitive to His Spirit as we should be, or we don't obey Him in the seemingly foolish things. The word of knowledge was moving nightly for a week of meetings. People were being healed and filled.

One afternoon I began having a sore spot on the bottom of the big toe on my (I think) right foot. It's been a whole year ago. The Lord said, "Call it out in the service tonight."

"I said, "God, I can't! What if no one has it? After all, a sore spot on the bottom of my big toe is too small and too foolish."

Who are we, anyway, to call foolish what God makes wise, or to call weak what He calls strong.

The Lord said, "Call it out."

"God, I can't," I said. "I just can't call out a sore spot on the bottom of a big toe!"

On the way home from the service that night I told the people I was with about the sore toe. The woman in the car covered her face with her hands and gasped.

"Oh," she said, between laughing and crying, "I sat with Mrs. in the nursery, and she said, 'You know, Betty calls out many things that a lot of us could have, and I know people are being healed of back problems and ulcers and things like that. But if she'd call out a sore on the bottom of the big toe of the right foot — about the size of a dime — I'd know it was for me!"

What a lesson I learned then. To be obedient when it seems ridiculous. To see God's tender care — yes, even for our toes. To trust Him utterly.

I know of no one in all the world through whom this gift flowed so wonderfully as it flowed through the ministry of Kathryn Khulman. Yet, she was the first to admit how human she was. She made mistakes. And some capitalized on her few mistakes rather than on the magnificent gift operating through her life by the Holy Spirit.

The person ministering in a small prayer group in Denver saw one serious back problem; the Holy Spirit saw three. Three men came forward in response to the word of knowledge and three men were healed and are still healed today seven years later.

A man and his wife came into a service one night. The man was in a wheel chair and had been there for several years, suffering from M.S. His wife was thin but attentive to him and concerned that he be healed. They were Baptist folks and believed in divine healing.

Everyone was praying for her husband to be healed. So was I, for my heart was touched. But suddenly the Holy Spirit directed my gaze from the man to his wife. It was as though she was illuminated in a bright light, God was so vitally interested in her needs. She was on the verge of a complete mental and physical breakdown. The load was too much. A full work load, plus caring for a sick husband, keeping house, — it was all rolling in on her at last. The husband was not looking for healing; he had accepted his condition. But his wife would go under the load if God did not touch her.

Leaving the platform to gently take her hand and pray for her, she began to weep as the word of knowledge came forth. A second or two later she went out under the power for twenty minutes. God, the Master Physician, did inner surgery on this Christian woman.

God reaches out. But individuals can accept or reject that word He gives. If they receive it, a healing takes place If they reject it, the word recedes back, so to speak, and it remains fruitless. Sadly, it is like a spiritual abortion.

Madame Guyon, 16th century Catholic was mightily used of God. She said If she spoke by the word of knowledge, results were immediate; if the word was rejected it came back to her.

We could liken that to the apostles being sent out into villages in the days of the early church. If the town received them, that town was blessed; but if the town rejected them, the apostles went to the edge of town and stomped the very dust of the place from their feet.

I took a woman's hand and spoke with her in the aisle about the occult which she and her husband were delving into in their country home. She flatly denied it. It was verified by the pastor and his wife after church. They rejected the word of knowledge, the Spirit who is all Truth, and remained in their present state.

Peter was right on target. *"Ananias, why hath Satan filled thine heart to lie to the Holy Spirit, and to keep back a part of the price of the land?"*

(Paraphrasing now) "While the land was in your possession you could do what you wanted to do with it. And after you sold it, you could do what you wanted to with the money from the land. But you promised to put the money into the common fund we have among us. You didn't have to lie about it. But now that you kept back part of the money for yourself, you've done something much worse than lying to us: you've lied to the Spirit of God!"

And Ananias was so terrified that his heart stopped beating and he died. The young men who were there wrapped him up and took him out and buried him.

Ananias' wife, Sapphira, didn't know what had taken place, but she was definitely in on the scheme to keep back a part of the money obtained from selling their piece of property. She came in about three hours later.

Peter said to her, "Tell me, did you sell the land for such and such amount of money?"

"That's right. That's what we sold it for."

And Peter said, "How can it be that you and your husband have agreed together to test the Spirit of God? Look, the feet of them who have buried your husband are at the door, and they shall carry you out also."

Sapphira fell dead at Peter's feet and she was buried beside her husband.

Peter was moving accurately. We, too, with proper teaching and waiting on God, can be that accurate today.

I prayed for a woman in a prayer line. "Do you have arthritis?" I asked.

"No, I don't," she replied.

I had been positive that arthritis had been there! A voice spoke from my left, a woman next to the one I had just spoken to.

"It's me," she said. "I have the arthritis." Well, I want to be more accurate than that. That doesn't satisfy me. God is accurate and He wants us to be accurate in all of our dealings in human lives, accurate in our work for His Kingdom. But when we do make a mistake, it shouldn't ever turn into a permanent sense of failure. No, we must strive to go on to perfection.

Perhaps, before reading this book, you never had a thought of whether or not the gift of the word of knowledge might be functioning in your life. Or maybe there were some of you who wondered about the gift and how you would know if it did operate. I certainly do trust that many of you are now correctly positioned in the Spirit of God to receive the flow and to know unmistakably whether the gift is moving out of your life or not.

The Bible tells us to "earnestly desire the best gifts. Therefore, it is quite right to pray for the word of knowledge to function through you. "But," some might ask, "How can we know whether or not that is one of the best gifts?" Well, if a gift can bring both inner and physical healings, if it brings joy, hope and encouragement, and if it can turn lives around and give direction and motivation, it must be a very wonderful gift indeed, — one of the best! If it is light streaming down from Him who is all light and truth to bring a captive out of darkness and put the enemy at bay, what a remarkable, yes, a magnificent gift it must be. It deserves top honors.

And if this gift should be brought into your life by the Holy Spirit, don't turn it away. Don't be afraid to let it move. God yearns to move and flow out of your life to extend a helping hand to someone in need. He will grant the knowledge, and He will take full responsibility to bring forth the fruit He desires. Just make yourself available to Him quietly and with confidence, and He shall grant the anointing and the direction He has for you.

www.ingramcontent.com/pod-product-compliance
Lightning Source LLC
Chambersburg PA
CBHW051208090426

42740CB00021B/3418